THE TRUTH ABOUT THE TAROT

THE TRUTH ABOUT THE TAROT

A Manual of Practice and Theory

by

Gerald Suster

SKOOB BOOKS PUBLISHING
LONDON

Published by:
SKOOB BOOKS PUBLISHING LTD
Skoob Esoterica Series
19, Bury Place
Bloomsbury
London WC1A 2JH.

ISBN 1 871438 07 1   Paperback.

Typeset by Shades and Characters Ltd.
Printed by Hillman Printers (Frome) Ltd.

FOR MICHAELA

and in memoriam
Candy Stapleton
1969~1990

CONTENTS

Author's Note

Throughout this treatise, the following equation of terminology between the Court Cards of the various Tarot packs is employed:—

Knight for King.

Queen = Queen.

Prince for Knight, in those packs wherein the Knight is the second male force.

Princess for Page.

Moreover, the traditional word 'he' has been used for the term 'any person', or 'he or she'. The present writer trusts that his woman readers will excuse his endeavour to evade cumbersome phrases, his sole motive herein. As will be discerned, a principal beauty of the Tarot is its expression of male and female equality.

G.S.

Preface

At a time when there are more books on the Tarot than shelf-space to store them, a work entitled simply THE TRUTH ABOUT THE TAROT might strike some as being an arrogant intrusion. That is for the reader to judge. The intention of this work is to do nothing less than live up to its billing.

It is written for the absolute beginner — and also for the most advanced students of the Tarot on the globe. I use the word 'student' in the sense it was used by one of the wisest men I ever met, my late, great friend, Dr. Israel Regardie (1907-85), psychologist, healer, magician and mystic. Although he enjoyed a wealth of more than fifty years' practical experience of the esoteric wisdom, whenever he was asked his 'grade' — a term signifying achievement and attainment — rather than lay open claim to Adeptship or Mastership, he always replied: 'I'm a student. We're all students.' Quite.

It was Socrates who declared: 'The more you know, the less you know.' I have found this to be Of All Truth in my own quest for truth, liberation and enlightenment, for life, love, liberty and light; which quest has mattered, does matter and will matter more to me than anything else in my experience. Such nuggets of wisdom I have gained I offer freely: but I have gathered them only because I knew what I did not know. As it is written in a noble document of enlightenment, *Liber Librae*: 'He who knoweth little, thinketh he knoweth much; but he knoweth much hath learned his own ignorance. Seest thou a man wise in his own conceit? There is more hope of a fool, than of him.'

My own commitments are to the raising of individual human consciousness and to the advancement of general human evolution during a period of the greatest crisis to confront Mankind on this planet for very many centuries. It is my conviction that the Tarot offers an invaluable, true, tried and tested Way of accomplishing these objectives.

Therefore my Will in the writing of this work is threefold:-
To give the novice every possible tool required for understanding and appreciation of and work with the Tarot as a noble route from the Earth to the Stars.

To share with my peers the learning, wisdom and perceptions I have gained from twenty-five years of continuous study and practice with the Tarot.

To entertain and delight those whose understanding of the Tarot may be in advance of mine.

We live in an extraordinary age of increasingly accelerating consciousness. Small wonder it is said that the Truth and the Tarot are many-splendoured things.

Foreword

Although I had been studying the basics of Comparative Religion since the age of ten, I knew nothing at all of the Tarot until I turned thirteen and came across it in a thriller, *The Devil Rides Out* by Dennis Wheatley. His description of those wholly unfamiliar visual images captivated my early adolescent consciousness, though I could not express just why I was so drawn to them, and they immediately inspired me to create my own pack. This was a most satisfying endeavour but I had no idea what to do with these strange pictures I had so crudely executed. There was within me a gut conviction that the symbols contained that wisdom after which I was seeking so confusedly and inarticulately — but I lacked all keys to understanding.

This prompted a period of furious reading. I bought and devoured every available work which might have bearing on the Tarot. For every volume which assisted me, there were at least ten which did not, for I was learning that the first virtue on the Path is Discrimination. However, I was amazed and delighted to discover, for instance, that the Tarot plays a vital part in what I still regard as being the most beautiful expression of human despair in the English language, *The Waste Land* by T.S. Eliot. By the age of fifteen, I was working with a traditional Tarot pack and undertaking occult experiments and mystical practices which augmented my comprehension, driven by a ravenous appetite which, as the Hindu proverb has it, provoked me 'to pant after wisdom as the miser pants after gold'.

As I continued to study the teachings and practise the disciplines of ways to enlightenment, the Tarot became my guide, philosopher and friend. I divined freely for anyone who requested it throughout my four years at Cambridge University. It was a joy to encounter the initial intellectual scepticism and subsequent surprised respect of my fellow undergraduates. Their fairness and the Tarot's accuracy have not been forgotten.

I have gone on working with the Tarot — and many allied ways to wisdom — throughout the fifteen years which have passed since my graduation, seeking all the while by its means to broaden and deepen my understanding of Man and his place in the Universe. Fortune has favoured me, for I have been enabled to walk and talk with students and scholars, with Adepts and Masters, with holy men and holy women of every Path: though all true Paths are One: and through our fruitful communication there has arisen greater comprehension.

Many books — far too many — have been written on the Tarot. Some are good but most are pointless. Why write another? And why do so when there already exists a masterpiece on the matter? I refer to The *Book of Thoth* by Aleister Crowley which, as he declares in the Bibliographical Note, 'was dashed off...without help from parents' to accompany the stunning Tarot deck he designed, painted exquisitely by Lady Frieda Harris. Here, all previous knowledge has been synthesised, married with the insights and inner knowledge acquired over a lifetime of spiritual exploration and devotion to the divine, and then set forth in a complex but beautiful system which is logically coherent and fits with the known facts about humanity and the Universe.

It is unnecessary to waste much time and space on defending Crowley who, among other things, was the greatest occult scholar and practitioner of our century. Twenty years of meticulous research support my inevitable conclusion that his 'evil' legend was — and is — a sordid mish-mash of malicious lies and disgustingly deliberate vilification. People who tell the truth are usually lied about and persecuted horribly — and so was he. The subject has been dealt with fully in my *The Legacy of the Beast* (W.H. Allen, London 1988; Samuel Weiser, Maine, USA, 1989) to which the interested reader is cordially invited to refer. The question before us is whether Crowley's work, developing as it does the synthesis of all past teachings accomplished by 'MacGregor' Mathers and the Hermetic Order of the Golden Dawn during the 1890's and from which well most subsequent authors have drawn without due acknowledgement, yes, whether Crowley's work has rendered subsequent efforts redundant.

Not so — if we judge simply by the sheer vast number of books on the Tarot published since Crowley's death in 1947. Are these really necessary? I think that some of them are. For Crowley makes few concessions to his readers, on whose part he assumes a highly educated background knowledge — with the predictable result that most beginners find *The Book of Thoth* to be virtually incomprehensible. As its author once wrote, in the manner of Robert Browning:

'It's rather hard, isn't it, sir, to make sense of it.' The same could of course be said of the major works of, say, Freud, Jung, Bertrand Russell, Wittgenstein or Einstein — who explored, *inter alia*, issues to be tackled later in this work. But this hardly helps the novice.

Secondly, as Crowley realised, the Tarot is an evolving tool capable of almost indefinite expansion. He himself made a major contribution in his relating of the Tarot to Qabalah, Astrology, Magick, Psychology and I-Ching, but much progress has been made in all these fields since his time. Global conditions have changed in a way he would barely recognise, attitudes have evolved, pioneers have discovered new techniques and advances of awareness have been attained in all the areas to which he directed our attention.

Crowley took Tarot from the Newtonian mechanics of predecessors such as Eliphas Levi, 'Papus' (Dr. Gerard Encausse) and the Golden Dawn, into the twentieth century relativism of Einstein.

For the present, though, it is not yet necessary for us to be concerned with the abstruse and the abstract. Theory means little in the absence of practice, which is exactly why the Introduction will be followed by things to do with the Tarot. Only when the reader is thoroughly familiar with the Tarot keys by dint of repeated usage with a variety of methods will he or she be able to embrace the Yoga of Knowledge. Furthermore, the contemplation of its celestial harmonies will add new dimensions to the perception of practical persistence.

Most people know that the Tarot is often employed for the purpose of vulgar fortune telling. Here you might be told that you will meet a tall, dark stranger of unique aspect who is devoted to music and desires much of great import from one who is worthy — and a few hours later you encounter a one-eyed, banjo-strumming busker with a bad case of sunburn who demands your money with foul-mouthed menaces. Although this work will give the student the means for going about trite operations of this nature, it is initially more concerned with proper divination, that is, the science and art of using the Tarot so as to perceive the forces of our past, the rhythms of our present and the probabilities of our future in terms of all we really want to do in Life.

However, divination is only one way of working with these wondrous keys to the Mysteries of Man and Nature. Others include the study of ancient knowledge contained in symbolism and mythology; psychology, physics, metaphysics and mathematics, of which the Tarot is a compendium; and the practice of esoteric disciplines, from Astrology to Qabalah, from I-Ching to meditation, from the art some know as 'scrying in the spirit vision' to the craft known by others as the subtlest game in the world.

For the Tarot is a genuine Way of developing the eight ninths of the brain which scientists declare to be unknown territory; of obtaining initiation into the great secrets of ancient times and the greater secrets of our own; and of bringing the body, imagination, intellect, emotions and sexuality; and the nervous system, cells and spirit to a god-like state of harmonious wisdom, love and power, that we may rejoice in our rapture as we experience our ecstatic union with our vast and starry Universe wherein we live and have our going.

Introduction

The Tarot is a pack of 78 cards. There are four suits: Wands, Cups, Swords and Disks. Each suit consists of cards numbered from Ace to Ten and four Court Cards: the Knight, the Queen, the Prince and the Princess. Our ordinary playing cards derive from the Tarot. There are also 22 'Trumps', numbered cards with curious pictures and titles like 'Death', 'The Devil', 'The Priestess', 'The Star', 'The Hermit' and 'The Lovers'. These are numbered from I to XXI apart from the card called 'The Fool', which is numbered 0 and has survived in our modern playing pack as The Joker.

The origins of the Tarot remain a mystery. Ancient Egypt, Sumeria, Morocco and even India have been suggested, and even insisted upon without any supporting evidence. It has been proposed by many authors that a group of sages or an individual sage wished to express universal truths in symbolic pictures which would survive the centuries. Possibly so: but all we know for certain is that the Gypsies brought the cards to Europe at some unidentifiable point prior to the fourteenth century and employed them for purposes of fortune-telling. In the late eighteenth century, French occultists claimed to discern hidden significance in the Tarot and its occult wisdom was insisted upon in the nineteenth century by the founder of its occult revival, Eliphas Levi, and then by his French successor, Dr. Gerard Encausse, in the latter's *The Tarot of the Bohemians*, written under the name of 'Papus'. There are few who find the work of Levi and Papus to be particularly helpful nowadays. The evidence suggests that Levi knew essential truths about the Tarot but was unable to tell them owing to oaths of secrecy he had sworn; and so there is little in his published work which can assist us here. For his part, Papus failed to put The Fool where any mathematician or person of common sense would have put a card numbered 0 — obviously at the beginning — and so succeeded in getting nearly every attribution wrong.

However, the collected perceptions of Levi and Papus, and also of their many associates and successors such as de Guiata and Sar Peladan and Huysmans — which galvanised French, English and German arts and letters 1880-1900 — undoubtedly influenced the next stage of research. Published writings, circulated manuscripts and repeated hearsay poured into the Hermetic Order of the Golden Dawn, which was founded in London in 1887. Its origins are not germane to this treatise. It suffices to state that it was a group dedicated to experiencing the Light of the Divine through development of the Self via sophisticated practices designed to enhance every human faculty. Its moving spirit, S.L. 'MacGregor' Mathers, consequently explored every method of enhancing human consciousness of which he was aware, synthesised Western and Middle Eastern wisdom traditions of the past 2500 years, and taught the resulting system to Golden Dawn initiates. The Tarot played a vital part in the Golden Dawn recension of pre-Christian wisdom as modified by 2000 years of slow rediscovery followed, after the Renaissance, by further experimentation and subsequent development.

This astounding compendium of esoteric learning and praxis can be studied with profit in *The Complete Golden Dawn System of Magick*, compiled, edited and commented upon by the late Dr. Israel Regardie. The history of the Order can be read in Regardie's *What You Should Know About the Golden Dawn*; *Modern Ritual Magic* by Francis King; and Ellic Howe's *The Magicians of the Golden Dawn*, which unites meticulous documentary research with a puzzling hostility to the author's subject matter.

Yet why is the Golden Dawn so important to a comprehension of the Tarot? After all, many authors have written on the matter without reference to its body of knowledge. That is precisely the point. There are writers on the Tarot who use it simply as a vehicle for expounding their own private convictions — this tells us much about them and with luck they give us individual insights into the Tarot, but we learn precious little else. We enter the world of a private individual and it may or may not be rewarding: we do not encounter the Universe. Other writers on the Tarot have devised systems to which the cards relate and which purport to explain the

Universe: here one tends to find that the internal logic of the system does not cohere and the presumed 'facts' contradict one's own experience of life. However, the vast majority of writers draw upon the Golden Dawn synthesis of age-old wisdom traditions, usually without acknowledgement; even so, let us enquire into the nature of this synthesis.

The Golden Dawn taught its initiates how to divine with the Tarot, the significance of its symbolism, its use in meditation, its employment for exploration of what some would term 'the Astral Plane', what Jungians would call the 'Collective Unconscious' and what we will name 'scrying'; and asserted that the Tarot is a pictorial exposition of the Qabalah.

This notion will be explored more fully in a later chapter. For the present it is enough to state that Qabalah is an extraordinarily sophisticated system of structuring the data of the Universe which is predicated upon Number, and upon the alleged affinity between Number and Letter, assuming the axiom that, as the Renaissance magus Dr. John Dee put it; 'Whatever is in the Universe possesses order, agreement and similar form with something else.' Qabalah came from the ancient Hebrew Rabbis, was taken up by non-Jewish pioneers and rediscoverers of wisdom during the Renaissance and has been developed further by their successors in the nineteenth and twentieth centuries.

The connection between the Tarot and the Qabalah has been disputed from two perspectives. One body of opinion, deriving from scholarly Judaism, deplores all departures from the orthodox Hasidic tradition but ignores the counter-arguments that the Qabalah, like the Tarot, is an evolving tool, intrinsically capable of almost infinite expansion. Others have denied all connection between Qabalah and Tarot on the grounds that there is no proven connection between the Jewish creators of the Qabalah and whoever was responsible for the Tarot.

It cannot be proved but it can be suggested that the Qabalah and the Tarot shared a common origin in Ancient Egypt. The symbol of the Sphinx on the Wheel of Fortune Trump in the medieval packs, long before the Sphinx was known in Europe, makes this plausible in the case of the Tarot. As for the Qabalah, it is believed to have originated with Moses, who received his education in Egypt and who, according to *The Bible*, became a most formidable Magician and a Mystic with direct access to God. It has been asserted also that the 22 Trumps were painted on the walls of one of the lower chambers of the Sphinx, though the present writer requires further evidence of this contention. Moreover, further research on the origins and travels of the Gypsies, who originally brought the Tarot to European attention, is obviously needed. Is there any genuine etymological connection between the words 'gypsy' and 'Egypt'; and if so, has it any material, historical significance? Only more research by open-minded scholars can confirm or disprove the Egyptian hypothesis.

Nevertheless, it can certainly be said that those who deny any connections between the Tarot and the Qabalah have seldom done any practical work with either. Moreover, those with practical experience of both declare the connection to be self-evident and concur with Crowley: 'The only theory of ultimate interest about the Tarot is that it is an admirable symbolic picture of the Universe, based on the data of the Holy Qabalah.'

This matter will be examined and set forth in due course: it is not a prerequisite for practice with Tarot. Nor is the next notion, expounded once again by the Golden Dawn, that the 22 Trumps represent the Twelve Signs and Ten Planets of Astrology.

The Tarot has also been shown to correlate, via the Qabalah, with that noble, ancient and extraordinary Chinese systemisation of wisdom, the I-Ching.

For the present, though, let us concentrate on basic practicality. You wish to know and use the Tarot? Very well: you will need a pack of Tarot cards. Having secured these, the first step is to get acquainted, for the cards are living beings, representing living forces in Mind and in Nature. Simply thumb through them and look at them.

There is no need for the present writer to imitate his predecessors and waste space and time by describing the cards: this seems a pointless exercise in view of the facts that the designs vary from pack to pack and moreover, you have eyes. As you regard the Tarot keys, quietly observe each detail of symbolism and note the thoughts and feelings, if any, which arise in you. In order to obtain maximum benefit from this and the ensuing exercises, you will need a notebook and pen. Every time you consult the Tarot, write down the date, the time, the duration of your consultation, the nature of the practice and any effect upon you. In this way, you will have a scientific record of your progress.

During this preliminary stage, be guided simply by your inclination. Observe which cards attract your attention and whether there are any you like or dislike — and try to analyse why. Some prefer to work and/or play with the Tarot simply when the mood takes them. The advantage of this approach is its spontanaeity. Its disadvantage is the curious psychological phe-nomenon, noted repeatedly in the work of all who seek to enhance the spirit: at first the practices seem easy and delightful; then they become an intolerably tedious chore; and in the end, a pristine pack of virtually unused Tarot cards lies neglected in a drawer, enlightening neither man nor beast. In fact, if one only persists through the customary period of boredom and disillu-sionment, a fresh state of mind arises whereby sessions with the Tarot take on new meaning and renewed joy. This is unlikely to occur if times for study and practice are governed by mood and whim: and that is why the traditional method tends to achieve more productive results.

This method consists of appointing a certain period of the day for work with the Tarot and keeping to that self-imposed resolu-tion. One should set oneself a realistic target which can be fulfilled without difficulty and which renders excuses ridiculous. Ten minutes a day for twenty-eight days is vastly preferable to an hour on the first day, thirty minutes on the second, five minutes on the third and a shiftless collapse for the rest of the month. Weariness is indeed likely to set in after the initial glow of pleasure but by virtue of simply keeping your word of honour to yourself on your promised timings, you will find a quiet pride, a growing mental strength and a developing perception until you break through to that exalted stage whereby the work goes of its own accord.

Which pack should you use? There are so many to choose from these days. One might well opt for something traditional. Nineteenth century French occultists scrutinised what was available, searching for a pack which expressed the most comprehensive compendium of symbolism. They chose one known as the Marseilles deck, which is old and crude but effective and appealing — and can still be readily obtained. This decision was wise, for then as now, there were decks which were drawn and painted well enough: but these amounted to little more than pretty pictures by professional fortune-tellers who may well have possessed predictive ability but who knew nothing of the Tarot's deeper significance. The so-called 'Swiss Tarot' and the Tarot of Etteila — pseudonym for one Aliette, an 18th century barber and clairvoyant — are classic examples of debasement. Nevertheless, it must be admitted that these and other packs can be used effectively for divinatory purposes: though the same is true of ordinary playing cards, a pool of ink in the palm of the hand or tea leaves.

The Marseilles Tarot can teach us rather more than tea leaves and one shares the respect paid to it during the nineteenth century and even now. Even so, it was certainly capable of improvement. Oswald Wirth, a French artist and occultist taught by Eliphas Levi designed a deck intended to clarify the symbolism, which Papus published alongside the Marseilles deck in his *The Tarot of the Bohemians*. This nineteenth century refinement has value and is available.

The Golden Dawn gave its initiates further and more complex teachings on the Tarot and set forth designs which summarised all knowledge within its portals. One initiate, A.E. Waite, later worked with the artist Pamela Coleman-Smith to create what became the best-selling Tarot pack in the world, marketed under the imprint of Rider. Whatever its virtues, it is not in fact faithful to the original Golden Dawn designs. Nevertheless, many find it to be their favourite: while others, such as the present writer, find it tame and twee, a charming version indeed but wholly lacking in force and fire, bearing the same relation to the mighty Universe as the enchanting, delightful but ultimately limited animated cartoons of Walt Disney.

The same can be said of the Paul Foster Case pack, which closely follows that of Waite. However, despite my reservations, the decks of Waite and Case are in the same class as that of Wirth and the Marseilles pack and are sound for our purposes if that is the reader's preference.

A deck based upon the original Golden Dawn designs has been issued. Israel Regardie acted as Consultant. The artist was Robert Wang, author of good books on the Tarot and Ritual Magic. The designs are commendable, as is the draughtsmanship, but the overall effect is weak.

In 1944, after five years of arduous labour, Aleister Crowley as designer and Lady Frieda Harris as Artist Executant published *The Book of Thoth*, though the cards were not issued as a pack until over twenty years later. As Crowley said of Harris: 'She accordingly forced him...to undertake what is to all intent an original work, including the latest discoveries in modern science, mathematics, philosophy, and anthropology; in a word, to reproduce the whole of his Magical Mind pictorially on the skeleton of the ancient Qabalistic tradition.' (Bibliographical Note to *The Book of Thoth*). It is the pack I would most strongly recommend. Here every line, every colour and every symbol is included for a specific reason guided by a central purpose and — one should add — so is every brush stroke. It is a great achievement.

This cannot be said of the many other Tarot decks which abound. The Aquarian Tarot has aesthetic merit but it is too stilted and pallid. The Tarot of Salvador Dali contains some beautiful examples of his work but tells us much more about the artist's private obsessions than it does about the Universe. The majority of packs have been created by people with little comprehension of the subject and can be dismissed as logically worthless and devoid of artistic appeal, the nadir being reached, perhaps, with the publication of *The James Bond Tarot*. The student would do far better to create his own, however crude, than employ a deck which misleads and offends.

Let us assume, therefore, that you have the pack you like most before you. At first it is best to regard them as just 78 interesting visual images which arouse varied reactions within you and for which great claims have been made but not yet proven. The next step is to sort them out. First, separate the 22 Trumps, or Major

Arcana, and place them in numerical order with The Fool — numbered 0 — at the beginning and The Universe — numbered XXI — at the end. Then arrange the Minor Arcana in the four suits of Wands, Cups, Swords and Disks; then put each suit in numerical order, from the Ten to the Ace and follow that with the Princess, Prince, Queen and Knight.

Having ordered your Tarot and put The Universe upon the Knight of Wands, in short, having imposed for the time being a structured pattern upon a random and chaotic Universe, you are now ready to try the exercise which draws most people to the Tarot.

Divination: and all that lies beyond it.

PART I

CHAPTER I

Divination

By understanding the forces of the past acting upon ourselves in the present, we can perceive probabilities for the future. The Tarot is a superb tool — some would say the finest — for doing this.

How does divination work? There are various theories to account for it. The traditional one was cogently expounded by Crowley.

'1. We postulate the existence of intelligences, either within or without the diviner, of which he is not immediately conscious. (It does not matter to the theory whether the communicating spirit so-called is an objective entity or a concealed portion of the diviner's mind.) We assume that such intelligences are able to reply correctly — within limits — to the questions asked.

2. We postulate that it is possible to construct a compendium of hieroglyphs sufficiently elastic in meaning to include every possible idea, and that one or more of these may always be taken to represent any idea. We assume that these hieroglyphs will be understood by the intelligences with whom we wish to communicate in the same sense as it is by ourselves. We have therefore a sort of language...better still is the analogy between the conventional signs and symbols employed by mathematicians, who can thus convey their ideas perfectly without speaking a word of each other's languages.

3. We postulate that the intelligences who we wish to consult are willing, or may be compelled, to answer us truthfully.'

(Magick: In Theory and Practice.)

A simpler theory is that there exists within the brain a faculty, often called 'clairvoyance', which can predict future probabilities and which is brought into play through a variety of tools: astrology, I-Ching, a crystal ball, tea leaves or the Tarot. Under this theory, the tools have little value in themselves and are there only to stimulate a part of the brain which we do not normally use.

A third theory was advanced by the psychologist Carl Jung; the theory of Synchronicity. Here it is argued that everything in the Universe is connected with everything else, so that laying our the Tarot cards will give us a picture of universal rhythms. Moreover, Jung posited the existence of the 'Collective Unconscious', that part of the mind which is common to all humanity, past and present, and which therefore contains the whole of human evolution and experience. This Collective Unconscious mirrors the external universe and manipulates our hands and fingers in the shuffling of the cards.

For the purposes of practical divination, it does not matter which of these theories is adopted. 'Who has the how is careless of the why.' And to begin with, divinatory work is mechanical. One starts with looking up the meanings of the cards in a book. Gradually, however, as you memorise the basic meanings then learn more of the cards' nature, you will find that the Tarot is working upon you and genuine insights into the situations you explore will arise spontaneously. A primary benefit of practising divination is the resulting development of your intuition.

Any system of divination requires method and meanings. There are very many methods from which to choose. The most complex is the Golden Dawn system, which Crowley reproduced in *The Book of Thoth*. Its advantage is its meticulous exploration of detail. Its disadvantages are that it is lengthy and cumbersome. Personally, I have never found it satisfying. For years I searched after a method that is simple, quick, direct and effective and eventually discovered it at the age of twenty-two, the number of the Tarot Trumps.

Here it is.

1. Think of a question. It can be as vague as: 'What are the general developments in my life over the next month?' It can be highly specific. Frame it clearly.

2. Shuffle the cards while concentrating exclusively on the question. If you are divining for another, then that person performs the mechanics.

3. When you have done with shuffling — go by feeling here — concentrate on the question one final time and cut with the left hand.

4. Lay out the cards as follows:

$$3$$
$$1 \quad 5 \quad 2$$
$$4$$

The fact that certain cards may be reversed plays no part in this method.

5. (1) is the influence coming into the matter. (2) is the influence in the process of departing from the matter. (3) is the most immediately apparent or conscious influence. (4) is the hidden, latent influence or subconscious factor. (5) is the key binding it all together.

6. Begin by interpreting with a work of reference which gives you the divinatory meanings. With practice, you will no longer need it.

7. Write down the interpretation as a series of statements. At the end, try to put all the influences together and summarise the position.

8. If you are dissatisfied with the result, do not ask the same question again on the same day. After all, one does not behave in this way to another human being: it is bad manners. However, do write down the divination in your Record.

9. When sufficient time has elapsed, mark your work for accuracy or lack of it. Let us say you have written ten statements. Has each statement turned out to be true or false? Give

yourself 1 for true and 0 for false. Tot up the marks at the end and express it as a percentage. At the end of, say, a year — though you could use three months or six months — average your percentages.

10. Do not be discouraged if your record of accuracy is initially poor. In the case of one diviner known to the present writer, a year's sincere, patient effort yielded a miserable mark of 35%. But a year later he achieved 85% and a year after that, 92%.

11. Do not fake your record in order to impress your acquaintances for you will only be cheating yourself and this may lead to the Tarot cheating you.
Sixteen years on, I still use this method.

What do the 78 cards mean? Let us take the Minor Arcana first. Much is sanctified by tradition, that is, a body of knowledge tried and tested over the centuries. However, in recognising the correspondences between the Tarot, Astrology and Qabalah, the Golden Dawn and Crowley refined this tradition and demonstrated its internal logic. Each of the cards from Two to Ten represents, among other things, the astrological influence of a particular planet in a particular sign.

The next idea to grasp is that of the Four Elements. Originally, many ancient mystery schools taught that everything is made up of three elements: Fire, Water and Air. Later they added a fourth: Earth. In the Tarot, Wands are Fire, Cups are Water, Swords are Air and Disks are Earth. Furthermore, Wands are Will, Cups are Love and Understanding, Swords are Mind and Conflict and Disks are Matter, including Money.

The Qabalah teaches that the Divine manifests through ten progressively more dense emanations of energy called Sephiroth, which are numbered from one to ten. Among other things, the Minor Arcana show how the four Elemental energies are affected by these succeedingly more material emanations. For instance, the Ace of Wands represents Fire and Will in absolute purity. These descend through the Sephiroth until a final degeneration in the Ten of Wands, which also represents Saturn in Sagittarius; the result is Oppression.

The following table sets out the meanings and the astrological correspondences:–

Wands

Ace = The Root of the Powers of Fire. Will.   *FIRE*
  2 = Dominion. Mars in Aries.
  3 = Virtue. Moon in Aries.
  4 = Completion. Venus in Aries.
  5 = Strife. Saturn in Leo.
  6 = Victory. Jupiter in Leo.
  7 = Valour. Mars in Leo.
  8 = Swiftness. Mercury in Sagittarius.
  9 = Strength. Moon in Sagittarius.
10 = Oppression. Saturn in Sagittarius.

Aries, Leo and Sagittarius are, of course, the three Fire Signs.

Cups

Ace = The Root of the Powers of Water. Supreme Love/Under-
      standing.
  2 = Love. Venus in Cancer.
  3 = Abundance. Mercury in Cancer.
  4 = Luxury. Moon in Cancer.
  5 = Disappointment. Mars in Scorpio.   *WATER*
  6 = Pleasure. Sun in Scorpio.
  7 = Debauch. Venus in Scorpio.
  8 = Indolence. Saturn in Pisces.
  9 = Happiness. Jupiter in Pisces.
10 = Satiety. Mars in Pisces.

Cancer, Scorpio and Pisces are the three Water Signs.

Swords

Ace = The Root of the Powers of Air. Clear Mind.
  2 = Peace. Moon in Libra.
  3 = Sorrow. Saturn in Libra.   *AIR.*
  4 = Truce. Jupiter in Libra.

5 = Defeat. Venus in Aquarius.
6 = Science. Mercury in Aquarius.
7 = Futility. Moon in Aquarius.
8 = Interference. Jupiter in Gemini.
9 = Cruelty. Mars in Gemini.
10 = Ruin. Sun in Gemini.

Libra, Aquarius and Gemini are the three Air Signs.

Disks

Ace = The Root of the Powers of Earth. Energy Earthed.
  2 = Change. Jupiter in Capricorn.
  3 = Work. Mars in Capricorn.
  4 = Power. Sun in Capricorn.
  5 = Worry. Venus in Taurus.
  6 = Success. Moon in Taurus.
  7 = Failure. Saturn in Taurus.
  8 = Prudence. Sun in Virgo.
  9 = Gain. Venus in Virgo.
10 = Wealth. Mercury in Virgo.

Capricorn, Taurus and Virgo are the three Earth Signs.

It remains to be added that our ordinary playing cards derive from the Tarot's Four Suits in the following way: Wands = Clubs; Cups = Hearts; Swords = Spades; Disks = Diamonds.

The Court Cards analyse the four Elements and the Holy Name of Tetragrammaton in the Qabalah; this latter will be dealt with in due course. For divinatory purposes, they describe various types of men and women. Crowley also gave them a coherent but extremely complex astrological attribution which few find to be especially helpful when divining. I shall therefore give a much simpler and cruder astrological attribution. This may appal the purist but many skilled diviners find that it works. The following consequently consists of this, the elemental analysis and a few psychological characteristics:–

Knight of Wands. Fire of Fire. A Fire Sign. A proud, generous, fierce and impulsive man. He can be cruel, bigoted and brutal.

Queen of Wands. Water of Fire. A Fire Sign. A proud, authoritative, strong-hearted, hot-tempered, loving woman. She can be vengeful, tyrannical, obstinate and savage.

Prince of Wands. Air of Fire. A Fire Sign, quite probably a Leo. A strong, swift, humorous, clever and noble man. He can be sadistic, callous, lazy and a braggart.

Princess of Wands. Earth of Fire. A Fire Sign. An energetic, violent, enthusiastic, implacable woman. She can be moody, unreliable, faithless and domineering.

Knight of Cups. Fire of Water. A Water Sign, quite probably Cancer. An extremely sensitive, amiable, innocent, graceful and passive man. He can be sensual, idle and a liar.

Queen of Cups. Water of Water. A Water Sign, quite probably Pisces. A dreamy, tranquil and gentle woman. She can be wholly lacking in character and initiative.

Prince of Cups. Air of Water. A Water Sign, probably Scorpio. An artistic, subtle, able and ruthless man. He can be irresponsible, secretive and devoid of conscience.

Princess of Cups. Earth of Water. A Water Sign. A gracious, sweet, romantic, voluptuous and tender woman. She can be selfish and lazy.

Knight of Swords. Fire of Air. An Air Sign, quite probably Gemini. A clever, skilful, fierce, delicate and courageous man. He can be violent for no reason, lacking in powers of reflection and incapable of purpose and decision.

Queen of Swords. Water of Air. An Air Sign. A perceptive, subtle, individualistic, confident and just woman. She can be cruel, sly and unreliable.

Prince of Swords. Air of Air. An Air Sign. An intensely intelligent man. He can be too intellectual, devoid of morality, impractical and wholly lacking in common sense.

Princess of Swords. Earth of Air. An Air Sign. A clever, practical, aggressive, stern and revengeful woman. She can manifest low cunning, anxiety and incoherence.

Knight of Disks. Fire of Earth. An Earth Sign, quite probably Virgo. A laborious, patient, instinctive, down-to-earth man. He can be dull, slavish and stupid.

Queen of Disks. Water of Earth. An Earth Sign, quite probably Capricorn. An intuitive, practical, quiet, hard-working, sensible and affectionate woman. She can be quietly debauched; and dull, servile and foolish.

Prince of Disks. Air of Earth. An Earth Sign, quite probably Taurus. An ingenious, energetic, capable, trustworthy, steady and thoughtful man. He can be insensitive, narrow-minded and resentful.

Princess of Disks. Earth of Earth. An Earth Sign. She contains all the characteristics of Woman but external influence determines which ones she manifests. She can be utterly inconsistent.

It will readily be observed that the bad qualities described in each case are a parody and degeneration of the good qualities. A good way of getting to grips with the Court Cards is to attribute them to each and every individual that you know. If the astrological method proves unsatisfactory, simply attribute in terms of qualities described. Try also to find the card which most accurately represents you and contemplate its visual imagery.

The Trumps are much more complicated and harder to understand, for they contain so much information that each one can be regarded as a book in itself. Nevertheless, for our present purposes, rapid advancement will be best achieved via a rough and ready simplicity. The following meanings will serve as a useful starting-point:–

0	*The Fool*	– chaotic experience; rapture and intoxication; wisdom in spiritual matters, folly in material; the agony and the ecstasy.
I	*The Magus*	– great intelligence; skilful manipulation.
II	*The Priestess*	– divine inspiration and/or blessing.
III	*The Empress*	– fruitful production through feminine influence or qualities.
IV	*The Emperor*	– Reason; male aggression and honour.
V	*The Hierophant*	– Intuition; the wisdom of age and of the ages.

VI   *The Lovers* – the union of opposites; or, indecision.

VII   *The Chariot* – triumph, but only if soft feminine qualities are employed within a hard, masculine exterior.

VIII *Adjustment* – Justice; essential balance, or failure to maintain it.

IX   *The Hermit* – Illumination from within; retirement, permanent or temporary; self-sufficiency; 'to thine own self be true.'

X   *Fortune* – Great good fortune if well-aspected; the reverse if ill.

XI   *Lust* – Courage, strength, energy. A great love.

XII   *The Hanged Man* – punishment, self-sacrifice, suffering.

XIII *Death* – A major transformation.

XIV   *Art* – Harmony between conflicting forces.

XV   *The Devil* – Immense force; blind impulse; eruption of animal instinct.

XVI   *The Tower* – Great conflict; sudden and devastating event or realisation.

XVII *The Star* – Hope and idealism fulfilled unless badly aspected, in which case heart-breaking disappointment.

XVIII *The Moon* – Illusion, fantasies, dreams and shadows unless well aspected; then 'the darkest hour before the dawn.

XIX   *The Sun* – Glory and great joy.

XX   *The Aeon* – Taking a definite step; the forceful resolution of the question.

XXI   *The Universe* – Persistence through difficulty if badly aspected. Otherwise, delight in the ordering of experience.

Students who use packs other than the Crowley-Harris deck should note the following equations in terms of Trump titles. The Magus = The Juggler or The Magician; The Priestess = The High Priestess or La Papesse; The Hierophant = The Pope; Adjustment = Justice; Lust = Strength; Art = Temperance; The Aeon = Judgement; The Universe = The World.

Two points must be borne in mind by the aspiring diviner. Firstly, each card is affected — i.e. aspected — and hence modified by the others on any spread. The diviner must therefore endeavour to transcend one's original, pedestrian, 'by the book' method through marrying the forces represented by the cards. This cannot be done intellectually, though it should be attempted at first; but only constant practice can supply the intuition necessary for this operation.

Secondly, the Tarot, in common with all divinatory systems, does not deal in certainties. If it did, there would be no free will at all and we would be programmed robots. Divination is about probabilities. Any given spread represents the ebb and flow of the Universe with regard to the particular situation under examination. Skilful divination consists of perceiving what is most likely to occur given the factors involved. This is why accomplished diviners are so accurate so often. However, the Universe is a much stranger place than is commonly supposed and as quantum physicists inform us, 'there is a factor infinite and unknown'. This is why even the most accomplished diviners are occasionally absolutely wrong.

There is much, much more to be learned about the meanings and use of the Tarot, all of which will greatly facilitate successful divination, but the present writer trusts that there is enough so far to enable the novice to essay this intriguing art; and that the more experienced of his readers will at least have drawn something useful from this chapter.

Constant practice of Divination not only develops the intuition but enables one to become aware of the flowing rhythms — and even quantum jumps — of the Universe and so to understand and appreciate our own divine place within it.

CHAPTER 2

The Royal Game of Human Life:
Or, Celestial Snakes and Ladders.

The first part of my title comes from Papus' *The Tarot Of The Bohemians*. Near the end, the author sets out a game to be played with the Tarot. It involves divination too. At first sight, it seems wholly fascinating and one would like to try it. Unfortunately, the author's instructions for playing 'The Royal Game of Human Life' are so unclear, that one regretfully concludes that it cannot be played or else is not worth playing.

Even so, I was inspired by the conception of a game with the Tarot. My desire to create one was further enflamed by Hermann Hesse's *The Glass Bead Game*. In this extremely interesting novel, wise men in an undated future express their wisdom and that of humanity by playing a game with glass beads. Each move represents a wave of thought or sensibility which affects all previous moves. Unfortunately, the author does not tell us how we can play it. It remains an ideal. However, there is merit in the notion therein that moves are judged not so much in terms of 'winning' and 'losing' but in terms of aesthetic play.

I invented a number of games with the Tarot, tried them on my friends, produced delight for a limited period in some cases but inflicted boredom in most, then withdrew in an endeavour to create another. Finally, and once again at the age of 22, I came up with a game which fulfilled all the criteria I had set myself and which was welcomed with enthusiasm. It is still being played in various parts of England, most notably London, and was recently introduced into California, where it has spread with gratifying swiftness. Many have asked me to codify the rules and to bring it to the attention of a wider public: I duly oblige.

Although the reasons for calling it 'The Royal Game of Human Life' or 'Celestial Snakes and Ladders' will become apparent, for the sake of simplicity, let us term it 'The Game'. The Game has five purposes.

1 – As an enjoyable and intriguing card game which can be played by anybody, whether a student of the Tarot or not.

2 – As the swiftest and most painless method of dynamically learning the correspondence between the Tarot and the Tree of Life, the diagram which summarises the Qabalah.

3 – As a complex but rewarding method of communication between players, suggesting Hesse's *The Glass Bead Game*.

4 – As a meditative method of learning about both the nature of the cards and one's own strengths and weaknesses.

5 – As a method of obtaining a divination for one's life at the point when the game is played, suggesting what can be extracted from Papus' *The Royal Game of Human Life*.

In order to play it, you will need a pack of Tarot cards and the diagram of the Tree of Life given in this book *(back page)*. This diagram shows the Ten Sephiroth of the Qabalah from 10 to 1 and the 22 Paths, represented by the 22 Trumps, which connect them. The next chapter on Qabalah will explain the theory of this diagram and also why Crowley changed certain Golden Dawn attributions but theory is not required for initial practice of The Game.

First look at the diagram. This is the map of The Game to which any player may refer at any time. You will be dealt eleven cards. The object is to play these cards and others you will acquire so as to ascend from 10 at the bottom to 1 at the top before any other player. You do this by playing your cards in numerical order, as in 10, 9, 8, 7, 6, 5, 4, 3, 2, Ace. So far, so uninteresting perhaps, but the Game has rather more to it. It is probably best understood if you play through a hand. If you have no one in the vicinity willing to be conscripted, simply deal out two sets of 11 cards for yourself and an imaginary player. The Game is for 2–7 people.

Look at your hand and arrange it in a way which satisfies you. It is prudent to put any Trumps to one side. Their extraordinary use will be explained. The so-called 'small cards' represent, obviously enough, the numbers they have on them. What about the Court Cards?

The Princess – 10.
The Prince – 9.
The Queen – 6.
The Knight – 1; and can be used as a wild card to substitute for ANY NUMBER. One could, for example, play a Knight for 10; hence the saying, 'a Knight to the rescue!'

Very well ; it is your go. A 'go' consists of any one of the following:–

1 – You build on your own pack. Each player has the pack he builds before him and therefore can observe the progress of the other players. In your case here, your aim is to get started by establishing yourself in 10. Therefore play a 10 or a Princess, or failing that, a Knight, if you have them. Place the card in front of you. OR —

2 – You can, in the future, accelerate your own progress up the Tree by playing an appropriate Trump on your pack. This remains to be explained. OR —

3 – Once your opponent(s) commences building his own Tree, you can impede it by placing an appropriate Trump on his pack. This remains to be explained. OR —

4 – If you can do none of the above, you may pick up the top card from the undealt pack. Then you must discard any card in your hand that you choose. This may be the card you have just picked up. You place it face up on top of the discard pile. OR —

5 – You may take the card face up on the discard pile and replace it with one from your hand. OR —

6 – You may open negotiations with any or all of the other players by asking for a card you need. No one has to deal with you and you don't have to deal with anyone else. A player may want a card you have in exchange. You do not have to state whether you have this card or not. However, all completed transactions must be by mutual consent and strictly honest. A completed transaction constitutes your go. If your negotiations yield no result, then you must exercise one of the options 1–5.

7 – Every go must end with you holding 11 cards in your hand. If you make a mistake, before you begin your next go, you start your turn by discarding if you have more than 11 or picking up if you have less.

Each player has a go in the above way. Let us suppose, then, that you have played a 10. The next step is to play a 9. But this is where the Trumps come in and the 'Ladders' aspect. It is possible to take short cuts. If you have The Moon, play that, for, as the 'map' shows, it will enable you to omit the playing of 9 and 8, and travel towards 7. If you have and play the Aeon, you may travel towards 8 without bothering with 9.

It is essential that the players grasp the notion of 'travelling towards'. The Trumps are not Numbers; they are paths *between* the Numbers. If you play The Moon from 10, on your next go you will be looking for a 7, and until you have played a 7, you cannot progress. Note also that there is no point in playing a Trump which is not a short cut at all. E.g. it would be a waste to play The Universe upon your 10 because after that, you would still be looking for a 9 anyway.

Good fortune in the hand could enable a lucky player to win very quickly via the following route: 10, 9, Art, 6, The Priestess, Ace — straight up the Middle Pillar. But games are only rarely as easy as that.

One major reason is the use of the Trumps as 'Snakes' or weapons. Suppose an opponent is at 9. You could place The Universe upon his pack. This would send him back to 10. Until he found and played a 10, he could not continue. Or you could be very pleased with yourself, having ascended from 10 to 8 via The Aeon, only for an opponent to knock you back towards 9 with The Sun.

You can use the Trumps to send opponents upwards and onwards only to encounter the disaster you planned. For instance, in one game, A was delighted, being established at 6, to have The Lovers placed upon his pack by B. This took him from 6 towards 3, which 3 he played on his next go. Unfortunately for him, B knocked him back towards 5 with The Chariot, and when he'd played a 5, towards 8 with The Hanged Man, and when he'd played an 8, she dropped him back towards 10 with The Aeon. It is an essential part of the spirit of the game to play it utterly ruthlessly and with no thought of personality. The word 'sorry' is allowed as Game etiquette but it often adds insult to injury.

The winner is the first player who can place an Ace on his pack. He or she then leaves the Game. If the others wish to continue, which is optional, the winner's remaining cards are added to the pick-up pile. If the player lacks an Ace, he may finish with a Knight, but he has not yet won for one round of goes. If during this round, anyone can place The Fool on his Knight, he is sent back towards 2.

The Fool has a unique function in the Pack. It is a completely wild card and can be played as a substitute for any Number or any Trump.

When the pick-up pack is exhausted, one simply turns over the discard pack, leaving the last card exposed.

If it is impossible for anyone to reach 1 and stalemate ensues, the winner is the player who has reached or is travelling towards the highest number.

The winner should closely scrutinise his winning pack before handing it in should other players wish to continue. And these other players should examine the packs that have been built at the conclusion of The Game. For each player will have acquired a divination of his state which should be read card by card, in chronological order, from the beginning to the end, as a story. The card on which one ends has the greatest importance for the immediate future.

The Game is in fact much less complicated than it seems at first. Most people pick it up easily in the course of their first attempt. In most cases, it grows on the player and reveals hidden depths. Organising a hand for maximum benefit becomes a subtle and meditative activity. One starts to perceive what is needed and what isn't at various stages of life and learning. The relations between the cards become increasingly apparent. Practised people play with wit and elegance.

Innovations to The Game have been proposed. One variant, which I heard about from Mr. David Rankine, brings in a mystical doctrine. The Numbers 1, 2 and 3 are held to be supreme and Ideal in the Qabalah, beyond the Abyss that yawns between Ideal and Actual. Anyone who reaches 2 or 3 must therefore give up his hand to the discard pile and receive 5 cards.

If he is brought down below 3 again, however, he is dealt another 6 cards. This innovation has its attractions but it remains to be seen whether or not it will pass into general play.

A technique of play some have criticised as pointless nevertheless deserves mention here, for it has been demonstrated to me as having a use. This consists of playing a Trump upon oneself when, to all intents and purposes, it is not needed. For instance, a player in 7 plays Death. This takes him travelling to 6, but he can go there by playing 6 anyway — so why do it? The reason is to avoid getting dragged away from 7 by another player. For example, while you are in 7 and looking for a 6, another might pick up and later play The Moon on you, sending you down towards 10. It is, then, a prudent move under certain circumstances, for when you are travelling upon a Trump, no one can play a card upon your pack.

It is to be hoped that The Game will bring many hours of pleasure and even more to readers who try it. Certainly it will accelerate comprehension of the immensely complex subject we are about to tackle, which subject is the backbone of the Tarot and the key to Understanding.

Qabalah.

CHAPTER 3

Qabalah

The contents of this chapter, though dry and detailed, are essential for any student who wants his understanding and usage of the Tarot to advance beyond the superficial. Practice is indeed the foundation of our kingdom, but in the absence of a unifying, guiding theory, its potential accomplishments are sadly limited. Hence it is strictly necessary at this juncture to tackle the matter of Qabalah.

What is Qabalah? One could do worse than give the answer of the late Dame Frances Yates:

'The Word means "tradition". It was believed that when God gave the Law to Moses He gave also a second revelation as to the secret meaning of the Law. This esoteric tradition was said to have been passed down the ages orally by initiates. It was a mysticism and a cult but rooted in the text of the Scriptures, in the Hebrew language, the holy language in which God had spoken to man.'

(The Occult Philosophy in the Elizabethan Age)

During the Renaissance, Qabalah became an integral part of its Hermetic Philosophy, the relevant parts of which can be summarised as follows:

1 – All is a Unity, created and sustained by God through His Laws.

2 – These Laws are predicated upon Number.

3 – There is an art of combining Hebrew letters and equating them with Number so as to perceive profound truths concerning the nature of God and His dealings with Man.

4 – According to the Qabalah, God manifests by means of ten progressively more dense emanations: and Man, by dedicating his mind to the study of divine wisdom, by refining his whole being and by eventual communion with the angels themselves, may at last enter into the presence of God.

5 – The Universe is an ordered pattern of correspondence: or as Dr. John Dee put it: 'Whatever is in the Universe possesses order, agreement and similar form with something else.'

(Gerald Suster: *John Dee: Essential Readings*)

We have noted how, in the late nineteenth century, S.L. 'MacGregor' Mathers welded together Renaissance occult philosophy, including and especially the Qabalah with certain of its sources which had come to light by his time in the creation of the Golden Dawn system. However, the practical use of Qabalah by Magicians and Mystics has still to be defined and in 777, Aleister Crowley gave the most succinct answer ever written.

'Qabalah is:

(a) A language fitted to describe certain classes of phenomena and to express certain classes of ideas which escape regular phraseology. You might as well object to the technical terminology of chemistry.

(b) An unsectarian and elastic terminology by means of which it is possible to equate the mental processes of people apparently diverse owing to the constraint imposed upon them by the peculiarities of their literary expression. You might as well object to a lexicon or a treatise on comparative religion.

(c) A system of symbolism which enables thinkers to formulate their ideas with complete precision and to find simple expression for complex thoughts, especially such as include previously disconnected orders of conception. You might as well object to algebraic symbols.

(d) An instrument for interpreting symbols whose meaning has been obscure, forgotten or misunderstood by establishing a necessary connection between the essence of forms, sounds, simple ideas (such as number) and their spiritual, moral or intellectual equivalents. You might as well object to interpreting ancient art by consideration of beauty as determined by physiological facts.

(e) A system of omniform ideas so as to enable the mind to increase its vocabulary of thoughts and facts through organising and correlating them. You might as well object to

18

the mnemonic value of Arabic modifications of roots.

(f) An instrument for proceeding from the known to the unknown on similar principles to those of mathematics. You might as well object to the use of $\sqrt{-1}$, x^4 etc.

(g) A system of criteria by which the truth of correspondences may be tested with a view to criticising new discoveries in the light of their coherence with the whole body of truth. You might as well object to judging character and status by educational and social convention.'

The formalised basis of the system is the diagram we have already encountered, the Tree of Life. This is a multi-purpose map. It can be used to classify states of consciousness, numbers, letters, colours, deities of every mythology, plants, jewels, the physical body, the Tarot or anything else in the Universe. It is a unifying symbol which embodies the entire cosmos.

It begins with Nothing, which is termed Ain. Ain is unknowable, unthinkable and unspeakable. To render Itself comprehensible to itself, Ain becomes Ain Soph (Infinity) and then Ain Soph Aour (Absolute Limitless Light) which concentrates itself into a central, dimensionless point. This point is called Kether and it is the first Sephirah (sphere) of the Tree of Life. The Light proceeds to manifest in nine more progressively dense emanations down to the tenth and final Sephirah, Malkuth, the physical world. This then, is how the Universe manifests, or how God or Goddess manifests, or how Darkness becomes Light and then Life — whichever terms are preferred — and it is held that every set of phenomena follows this pattern. This is why the Tree of Life is viewed as a multi-purpose map.

So our map so far consists of ten Sephiroth. These Sephiroth are connected by twenty-two Paths which express the relations between the Sephiroth they connect. The original creators of the Qabalah attributed the twenty-two letters of the Hebrew alphabet to these Paths and connected them with a symbol, the Serpent of Wisdom, who includes all Paths within its coils as it climbs from the lowest to the highest.

This system has been further expanded and made more complex over the centuries. It is held by most Qabalists that there are

19

Four Worlds, or dimensions of existence, and each World has its own Tree of Life. Many go further and work with a system whereby each Sephirah contains a Tree, giving us a total of a hundred Trees or, if we bring in the Four Worlds, four hundred. These refinements are beyond the scope of this work but can certainly be studied with advantage in *The Mystical Qabalah* by Dion Fortune or Israel Regardie's *A Garden of Pomegranates*.

It should be added, however, that there are two ways of regarding Qabalah. The traditionalists believe that the Tree of Life is the actual framework of the Universe. Crowley disagreed and commented acidly:

'It was as if some one had seriously maintained that a cat was a creature constructed by placing the letters C.A.T. in that order. It is no wonder that Magick has excited the ridicule of the unintelligent, since even its educated students can be guilty of so gross a violation of the first principles of common sense.'

(Magick: In Theory and Practice.)

His point was that the Tree of Life is a *classification* of the Universe, not a thing in itself. Its unique advantage, as Mathers, Crowley, Regardie, Fortune and other Qabalists insist, is that it is the most supple, comprehensive, ingenious and most useful tool of universal classification that the mind of man has ever invented.

During the 1890's, Mathers proceeded to write Tables of the Tree of Life to classify his vast occult knowledge. Dr. Wynn Westcott very probably assisted him and these Tables were circulated among Inner Order initiates, including Crowley's teacher, Allan Bennett. Bennett was an excellent Qabalist in his own right and Crowley learned from him, then acquired his own experience. A most fruitful result was the publication in 1909 of 777, the classic dictionary of correspondences, which most subsequent writers have plundered without acknowledgement. As Crowley wrote in his Preface:

'The following is an attempt to systematise alike the data of mysticism and the results of comparative religion...for us it is left to sacrifice literary charm and even some accuracy, in order to bring out the one great point.

'This: That when a Japanese thinks of Hachiman, and a Boer of the Lord of Hosts, they are not two thoughts, but one.'

The main Tables are based on thirty-two numbers: that is, the ten Sephiroth and the twenty-two Paths. If we look at the correspondences pertaining to the number Twelve, for example, we will find that the Planet is Mercury, the Path joins the Sephiroth 1 and 3, the foremost colour is yellow, the Egyptian God is Thoth, the Hindu deity is Hanuman, the Greek God is Hermes, the Roman God is Mercury, the animals are the Swallow, Ibis, Ape and Twin Serpents, the plants are Vervain, Herb Mercury, Marjoram and Palm, the gems are the opal and agate, the magical weapon is the Wand or Caduceus, the perfumes are Mastic, white sandal, mace and storax, the metal is mercury, the Hebrew letter is Beth and the Tarot Trump is The Magus. One could say that The Magus is a pictorial representation of all these associated ideas.

One uses 777 or an equivalent work to set up magical ceremonies, to guide one in meditation and/or to compare systems of symbolism and mythology. Once its basic principles are comprehended, one can classify new knowledge.

We must now briefly turn our attention to what is known as Gematria, a way of 'combining Hebrew letters and equating them with Number so as to perceive profound truths concerning the nature of God and His dealings with Man.' Specifically, Gematria is the art of discovering the secret sense of a word by means of the numerical equivalents of each letter. As Regardie states in *A Garden of Pomegranates*:

'Its method of procedure depends on the fact that each Hebrew letter had a definite numerical value and may actually be used in place of a number. When the total of the numbers of the letters of any one word were identical with that of another word, no matter how different its meaning and translation, a close correspondence and analogy was seen.'

He gives us an interesting example. The Hebrew of 'Serpent' adds to 358 and so does the Hebrew for 'Messiah'. This may initially appear rather surprising but close inspection and a further operation of Gematria will clarify the matter. For what is the Serpent? As Regardie puts it: 'The Serpent is a symbol of the Kundalini, the spiritual creative force in each man which, when aroused by means of a trained will, re-creates the entire individual, making him a God-Man.' And the Messiah is a God-Man.

Furthermore, if we add up the digits 3, 5, 8, we obtain 16, and if we look up the correspondences of that number in 777, we find Dionysus the Redeemer — and the Tarot Trump The Hierophant, divine and human initiator into the sacred mysteries of realising one's own innate divinity. Another correspondence is that of Parsifal, who like The Hierophant, becomes able to perform the messianic miracle of redemption. As Regardie rightly states: 'We thus see the specific analogy between the words 'Serpent' and 'Messiah' which the Qabalah has been able to reveal.'

Crowley gives us further examples in *The Book of Thoth*:

'For example, AChD unity (1 + 8 + 4) = 13; and the AHBH love (1 + 5 + 2 + 5) = 13. This fact is held to indicate "The nature of Unity is Love." Then IHVH Jehovah (10 + 5 + 6 + 5) = 26 = 2 x 13. Therefore: "Jehovah is Unity manifested in Duality.'

Let us take the Number 419. It is a prime. What can we learn of it? Investigations will probably prove futile until we hit the key realisation that it is the number of the Hebrew Letter Teth spelled in full. And Teth corresponds to the Tarot Trump Lust. We can therefore explore the nature of 419 by meditating upon this Tarot Trump and its various correspondences.

The student who wishes to investigate further the fascinating science and art of Gematria should obtain *The Qabalah of Aleister Crowley*, which volume contains his three major contributions to Qabalah: Gematria, 777 and *Sepher Sephiroth*. This last volume is a dictionary of Hebrew words arranged according to their numerical value. Gematria also investigates the characteristics of many numbers. You can then look up the properties of any number. If you wish to investigate a word, change it into Hebrew letters, add up the numerical equivalents of these letters and refer to the book for the meaning or meanings. If at first this sheds little light upon the path, divide the number you have and inspect the meanings of the factors. Remember that you can substitute the appropriate Tarot Trump if a Number is between and including 11 (The Fool) and 32 (The Universe). If the result is still less than satisfactory, try adding up the digits. Tarot, then, can assist us in our comprehension of Gematria, which, one has to admit, at first strikes the casual reader as absurd. Yet anyone who undertakes its practice will come to agree with Crowley:

'Complete mystery surrounds the question of the origin of this system; any theory which satisfies the facts demands assumptions which are completely absurd. To explain it at all, one has to postulate in the obscure past a fantastic assembly of learned rabbins, who solemnly calculated all sorts of combinations of letters and numbers, and created the Hebrew language on this series of manipulations. This theory is plainly contrary, not only to common sense, but to the facts of history, and to all that we know about the formation of language. Nevertheless, the evidence is equally strong that there is something, not a little of something but a great deal of something, a something which excludes all reasonable theories of coincidence, in the correspondence between words and numbers.'

(The Book of Thoth.)

For it must be stressed that Qabalah is usually found as meaningless as Higher Mathematics by those with no practical experience of the subject. One cannot learn Qabalah simply by reading about it any more than one can learn chemistry without ever entering a laboratory and performing an experiment. Understanding depends upon and grows with honest work.

Now, even the dullest student cannot fail to have noticed how neatly the Qabalah and the Tarot fit together. There are ten Sephiroth and Four Worlds — and four suits of ten cards numbered from 1 to 10. There are 22 Paths, 22 Hebrew letters — and 22 Trumps. Qabalah begins with 0 — and so does the Tarot with The Fool. Furthermore, if one looks up the Egyptian, Greek and Roman Gods and Goddesses for numbers 11–32 inclusive in 777 or an equivalent, one will find these reflected in the corresponding Tarot Trumps. One could adduce many other considerations and continue at intolerably wearisome length, citing parallel after parallel;

and opponents of this position have yet to explain these parallels satisfactorily. But the central point is that those who work with both Qabalah and Tarot find the connections to be self-evident.

It has been objected by some authors on the Tarot — and they ought to know better — that connecting the Tarot to the Qabalah, or any other systemisation of knowledge and wisdom, is 'dogmatic' and even 'anti-tarotic', whatever that last phrase may mean. This attitude displays a dismal paucity of ratiocinative faculty. One of the many joys of the Tarot is that it can increase our understanding and appreciation of so many other ways of structuring the Universe.

In common with the Tree of Life it portrays, the Tarot is a multi-purpose tool and a multi-faceted map. Many get to grips with Qabalah through the Tarot rather than vice-versa, for they find they respond better to visual imagery than to the abstractions of Number. For instance, on the Tree of Life the seventh Sephirah is Netzach, the tenth Sephirah is Malkuth, and these are connected by the twentieth Path, which expresses the relations between them. How is one to comprehend the nature of this relationship?

A pure Qabalist, after looking up any correspondences he had not already memorised, would probably begin by studying the meaning of the Hebrew letter Qoph; this means 'Back of head' in English, which clearly refers to the cerebellum or primitive reptile brain and all that this implies; after which he would probably explore all relevant numbers. But one who approached the matter via the Tarot would first study the Tarot Trump numbered XV, The Moon, to which the Path is attributed, and might well find that the visual symbol and the trains of thought it evokes grant greater comprehension than intellectual abstractions. Obviously a thorough seeker after wisdom would study the matter from both aspects. Through the one, we can gain increasing perception of the other and vice-versa. The student must remember that each Tarot card is not called a 'key' for nothing, for each one is a compendium of associated ideas, represented by symbolism.

We again find the Tarot to be of invaluable assistance in endeavouring to comprehend the nature of that Divine Name studied and revered by Qabalists, Shemhamphorash, which expresses what is known as the Formula of Tetragrammaton and which, when pronounced correctly, is alleged to destroy the Universe — or, one might say, annihilate the personality through immediate contact with the divine. It is not the purpose of this treatise to enter deeply into this particular subject but an elementary sketch of the formula of Tetragrammaton is necessary.

Tetragrammaton can be described as the Four Letters of the Divine Name of God: IHVH which in Hebrew is Yod Heh Vau Heh, usually vulgarised as Jehovah. These letters are portrayed as Father, Mother, Son and Daughter. In the traditional Hebrew system, the divine forces symbolised by the Father (Active) unite with the Mother (Passive) to produce Matter in the form of the Son and the Daughter.

The Pagan system is subtler and more in accord with our contemporary knowledge of the Universe. It encapsulates the equation 'Naught = Many = Two = One = All = Naught' which can be reduced to $0 = (+1) + (-1)$, or in shorthand, $0 = 2$. In other words, Nothing manifests through various processes as Everything through Pairs of Opposites. One way of expressing the process is to say that the Father (Yod) and Mother (Heh), from whom issue all created things, unite to bring forth the Son (Vau) who is the heir, and then the Daughter (Heh). Through his bravery, the Son wins the Daughter in marriage, and she is set upon the throne of her Mother. She then awakens the Eld of the original Father who becomes the young Son while the Son takes his Father's place — and the cycle is renewed. As Crowley remarks:

'In this complex family relationship is symbolised the whole course of the Universe.'

(Magick: In Theory and Practice)

This formula has many and varied applications to Magick and Mysticism and Life generally and these can be studied in the relevant specialist works. What is presently germane to our purposes is that we find this Formula embodied in the Court Cards of the Tarot. The Knight is the Father; the Queen is the Mother; the Prince is the Son; and the Princess is the Daughter.

25

Contemplation of these keys will immeasurably assist comprehension of the immensely complex and powerful wisdom enshrined in Tetragrammaton. For these mystical formulae can only be grasped to a limited degree through purely rational analysis. Through Tarot — and Qabalah — we can acquire another highly effective way of using our brains. 'Associative thinking' might be one way of describing it, 'lateral thinking' another, though both these terms are inadequate.

Our next consideration is Daath. This is the eleventh Sephirah of the Tree of Life and has hitherto not been mentioned. It plays little part in the traditional system. The orthodox Hebrew qabalists thought that, properly speaking, it was not really a Sephirah at all. Recent times, however, have witnessed great interest in Daath and the matter has been explored in the works of Mr. Kenneth Grant, and those influenced by them. The place of Daath is in the Abyss, between 3 (Binah) and 4 (Chesed) and 2 (Chokmah) and 5 (Geburah). Tradition has it that it means Knowledge but is in fact the False Crown of False Knowledge. It represents, it is said, the highest state to which a human being can bring his intellectual faculties and spiritual evolution without doing what he then must do — give up all that he has and all that he is, annihilating his self in a mystic marriage with the Universe. To stay in the state of Daath, it is said, is to cling to one's ego and to be destroyed.

A number of contemporary writers such as Mr. Grant have argued vehemently for a revision of this position. They point out, among other things, that the Hebrew Rabbis were riddled with guilt; that the number of Magick is 11 and so the Tree of Life should reflect this with 11 Sephiroth; and that Daath, far from being a False Crown of False Knowledge, is the Gateway through the Abyss to Binah (Understanding) and the birth within us of cosmic consciousness.

In the opinion of the present writer, the significance of Daath is still a matter for debate and will only be resolved by patient study and experimentation, though the latter may lead to casualties. The matter is mentioned here so as to enable the student to get to grips with recensions of the Tree of Life based on eleven

Sephiroth; and to have a basis for understanding material to be presented in the succeeding chapter on Astrology.

Penultimately, two more technical matters demand our attention. Firstly, although the Marseilles deck had Justice at VIII and Strength at XI, why did Waite and Case counterchange them, and why did Crowley revert to the traditional attribution? At first inspection, it looks as though Waite and Case were right. A Lion usually appears on Strength, which therefore obviously refers to the Astrological Sign, Leo; a woman with sword and scales usually appears on Justice, and this obviously refers to the Astrological Sign of Libra, the Balance: and in the Zodiac, Leo comes before Libra.

Crowley was at first perplexed by the traditional ordering. However, in 1904 he received *The Book of the Law*, which at the very least is an intensely beautiful prose-poem announcing a new Aeon of evolution for humanity and which he asserted to have been dictated to him by a praeter-human Intelligence called Aiwass. With reference to the Tarot, *The Book of the Law* states: 'All these old letters of my book are aright; but Tzaddi is not the Star. This also is secret; my prophet shall reveal it to the wise.' In other words, the Hebrew letter Tzaddi and the Path to which it is attributed do not correspond to the Trump numbered XVII The Star, contrary to Golden Dawn teaching. As Crowley comments:

'This was exceedingly annoying. If Tzaddi was not "The Star", what was? And what was Tzaddi? He tried for years to counterchange this card, "The Star", which is numbered XVII, with some other. He had no success. It was many years later that the solution came to him. Tzaddi is "The Emperor"; and therefore the positions of XVII and IV must be counterchanged. This attribution is very satisfactory...

'For "The Star" is referred to Aquarius in the Zodiac, and "The Emperor" to Aries. Now Aries and Aquarius are on each side of Pisces, just as Leo and Libra are on each side of Virgo; that is to say, the correction in the *Book of the Law* gives a perfect symmetry in the zodiacal attribution, just as if a loop were formed at one end of the ellipse to correspond exactly with the existing loop at the other end.

27

'These matters sound rather technical; in fact, they are; but the more one studies the Tarot, the more one perceives the admirable symmetry and perfection of the symbolism. Yet, even to the layman, it ought to be apparent that balance and fitness are essential to any perfection, and the elucidation of these two tangles in the last 150 years is undoubtedly a very remarkable phenomenon.'

(The Book of Thoth)

In other words we obtain a symmetrical, balanced and satisfying systemisation of Tarot in terms of all it expounds, if we place Adjustment (Justice) at VIII and Lust (Strength) at XI; and if we attribute the Hebrew letter Tzaddi and the Path between 9 (Yesod) and 7 (Netzach) to IV The Emperor; and the Hebrew letter Heh — The Great Mother and the Great Daughter — and the Path between 6 (Tiphareth) and 2 (Chokmah) to XVII The Star.

This latter counterchange also makes sense in terms of our growing comprehension of enlightenment during the age in which we live. Under the traditional system, the way of spirit from 6 (Tiphareth — Beauty) to 2 (Chokmah — Wisdom) was thought to be via the Path of The Emperor, who among other things symbolises the mighty male ruler, the All-Father, Jehovah. The Star was thought to symbolise just the passing from 9 (Yesod — Foundation — the Subconscious and Imagination) to 7 (Netzach — Victory — Emotion), exalted though that passing is. Crowley must have been intuitively dissatisfied with this, for in his beautiful and haunting fairy tale *The Wake World*, written before he finally accepted *The Book of the Law* in 1909, although he employed the traditional attributions in his story of the ascent of the human soul from the dross of the human to the fire of the divine, he nevertheless hinted at the realisation that The Star portrays the Great Goddess.

'Then there was another passage which was really too secret for anything; all I shall tell you is, there was the most beautiful Goddess that ever was, and she was washing herself in a river of dew. If you ask what she is doing, she says: "I'm making thunderbolts." It was only starlight, and yet one could see quite clearly, so don't think I'm making a mistake.'

(From *Konx Om Pax*)

Today most seekers realise the nature of the evils which authoritarian patriarchy has wrought upon the Earth and can apprehend the greatness of the Goddess in the Earth, the Moon and above all, the stars. Crowley's counterchange is therefore singularly appropriate. Instead of the worst aspect of The Emperor leading us to cosmic consciousness, a fierce, jealous and bloodthirsty father-figure roaring: 'Don't argue! Do as I say!' there is the Star Goddess compared to whom one's ego is but a grain of dust but whose nature is Love and who enchants us with her cry: 'To me! To me!'

Likewise, instead of the worst aspect of The Star leading us from the personal subconscious, including its ills, to the experience of genuine emotion by means of self-pity, self-indulgence and a cry for an all-forgiving mother-figure, there is instead the strong, masculine force of The Emperor to remind us of the needs for self-discipline, reason and will if this transition is to be successfully accomplished.

The present writer has never seen the point of plagiarism or of tampering with words which cannot be bettered. This is therefore an opportune moment to quote Crowley's 'Summary of the Questions Hitherto Discussed.'

'1. The origin of the Tarot is quite irrelevant, even if it were certain. It must stand or fall as a system on its own merits.

2. It is beyond doubt a deliberate attempt to represent, in pictorial form, the doctrines of the Qabalah.

3. The evidence for this is very much like the evidence brought forward by a person doing a crossword puzzle. He knows from the "Across" clues that his word is "SCRUN blank H"; so it is certain, beyond error, that the blank must be a "C".

4. These attributions are in one sense a conventional, symbolic map; such could be invented by some person or persons of great artistic imagination and ingenuity combined with almost unthinkably great scholarship and philosophical clarity.

5. Such persons, however eminent we may suppose them to have been, are not quite capable of making a system so

abstruse in its entirety without the assistance of superiors whose mental processes were, or are, pertaining to a higher Dimension.'

So in addition to our practices of Divination and the Royal Game of Human Life, we also have a map. Its further details will be made known to us only through further study and experience. A vital key here is meditation, which will form the subject of a later chapter. Each card and the multifarious ideas associated with it, must be revolved through the mind again and again and again. In the end, any card should trigger a stream of living correspondences: and this is rather like acquiring a new brain.

For the present, though, the student is invited to try a series of abstract meditations based upon Crowley's 'Naples Arrangement', the simplest recension of how the manifested Universe came to be as expressed through the schema of the Tree of Life. It consists of thirteen separate meditations to be done for thirteen days at a minimum of five minutes a day. Simply sit with a straight back in an upright chair, concentrate one-pointedly on the following and record the results.

0 Contemplate Absolute Nothing.
0 Contemplate Space, Infinity.
0 Contemplate Limitless Light as a basis of a possible vibration.
1 Concentrate on an indefinable Point.
2 Concentrate on a Line which connects two Points.
3 Concentrate on a Triangle. The original Point is now defined by relation to two others.
4 Go from two to three dimensions. Concentrate on Matter. What is it?
5 Events can only occur through Motion and in Time. Concentrate on Motion and Time. What are they?
6 Concentrate on a Point which is conscious of itself in terms of itself, another point, another two points, Matter and Time and Motion. In other words, it lives, moves, has its being and knows it.
7 Concentrate on this Point's Idea of Bliss.
8 Concentrate on the Point's Idea of Thought.
9 Concentrate on the Point's Idea of Being.

10 Concentrate on this Point fulfilling itself by its experience of 7, 8 and 9 simultaneously.

This is not an easy series of exercises but experience with the hardest, however arduous, will stand one in good stead for obtaining maximum benefit from less demanding practices. What is being essayed here is no more and no less than a realisation of how one came to be.

Although this series of exercises is exceedingly simple and direct, this is precisely the principal disadvantage for most people. The majority may well get nowhere with it. This is yet another reason why the Tarot is so indispensable a tool. Its very complexity stimulates the student, enabling him to apprehend at last the supreme simplicity of the Universe.

NOTE

The technically minded may find that there is still some confusion pertaining to the counterchange outlined in this chapter between Adjustment and Lust; and The Emperor and The Star.

In the opinion of the present writer, those working with the Tree of Life should attribute Adjustment (Justice) to the Hebrew Letter Lamed and the Number 22 on the Key Scale of 0–32; Lust goes with Teth and 19. The Emperor being Tzaddi — a root of the words Tzar, Caesar, Seigneur etc — is attributed to 28 on the key scale; and The Star to 15 (Heh).

The result is balance.

CHAPTER 4

Astrology

As previous chapters have shown, the Tarot corresponds with Astrology, both in itself and via the Tree of Life. Anyone with knowledge of Astrology will find that it augments comprehension of the Tarot and vice-versa. Let us therefore regard the various correspondences, starting with the twelve Signs of the Zodiac:–

Aries the Ram is represented by IV The Emperor, who is usually portrayed with a ram or a ram's head.

Taurus the Bull equates with V The Hierophant. Students of mythology may recall the function of the bull as Redeemer in the mysteries of Apis and Mithras. *HIGH PRIEST.*

For Gemini the Twins, we have VI The Lovers.

Cancer the Crab is represented in the Tarot by VII The Chariot.

Leo the Lion is represented by XI Lust, on which a lion or lion-like beast is usually depicted. Logically we should expect to find this key at VIII, which is why Waite and Case put it there. However, although this imparts a neater sequence of astrological attributions, it does not fit with others. Astrological considerations have therefore been sacrificed to a greater cause. In any case, the reasoning of the matter has been dealt with in the previous chapter. *STRENGTH.*

Virgo the Virgin is shown in the Tarot by IX The Hermit.

Libra the Balance is VIII Adjustment, usually portrayed with sword and balance. *JUSTICE.*

Scorpio the Scorpion is symbolised in the Tarot by XIII Death.

Sagittarius the Archer equates with XIV Art in the Tarot. The bow and arrow stand for the union of male and female, pictured in most Tarot decks by a woman or hermaphrodite mixing two different substances. *TEMPERANCE*

Capricorn the Goat is appropriately portrayed in the Tarot as
   XV The Devil.
Aquarius the Water Bearer is pictured in the Tarot by XVII The
   Star, in which a woman or Goddess bears and pours water.
Pisces the Fish is represented in the Tarot by XVIII The Moon.

Let us now turn to the 7 Planets known to the Ancients.
The Sun is obviously represented by XIX The Sun.
Mercury is portrayed by I The Magus. MAGICIAN .
Venus is pictured by III The Empress.
The Moon is shown by II The Priestess.
Mars is XVI The Tower.
Jupiter is X Fortune.
Saturn is XXI The Universe.

There is some difficulty when we turn to the remaining three
cards. Traditionally, they were thought to equate with the original ancient theory of all being composed of three Ideas or
Elements: Air (The Fool), Water (The Hanged Man) and Fire
(The Aeon). A problem arose with the positing of a fourth Idea
or Element, Earth, and so in some systems, The Universe had to
do double duty for this and Saturn, demonstrating the intimate
connection between the farthest known planet and our own as in
the saying 'As above, so below.' An alternative was to let the
Four Elements of the Minor Arcana represent Earth. However,
the whole matter had to be revised in view of the astronomical
discoveries of Uranus, Neptune and Pluto. The present position
gives the following attributions:–
   Uranus –   XX The Aeon.
   Neptune – XII The Hanged Man.
   Pluto –   0 The Fool.
This will do for the present but the student is earnestly
cautioned against accepting it too readily. Let him remember
that our understanding of the Tarot is still evolving, which is one
of the principal joys of the subject.

What can we actually do with these equations? We can increase our understanding of various matters through, for
instance, the performance of three interesting exercises.

A ~ Relating Astrology and Tarot.

1 – Obtain a good, short primer on Astrology, one which does little more than set out the basic meanings of the Signs and Planets.

2 – Learn how to draw the astrological symbols. A working knowledge of these glyphs is useful and enlightening.

3 – Apply your astrological knowledge to the relevant Tarot keys. Take it a Sign at a time, then a Planet at a time.

4 – Note how your knowledge of the Sign/Planet is similar to or different from the Tarot key you examine. How do the symbols express the astrological information? Is there anything there which adds to your knowledge?

5 – Do not be too perplexed if at times, in the course of your meditation, you encounter contradictions. One lesson taught by the Tarot is that every idea contains within itself the seed of its own opposite.

B ~ Help for a Horoscope.

1 – Obtain a short, simple primer which instructs you on how to set up a horoscope and do so for yourself. Probably you will also need a set of astrological tables. Alternatively, obtain your horoscope from an astrologer friend or a commercial service which employs a computer and charges reasonably.

2 – Try to interpret the data with the aid of your Astrology primer. Record the results.

3 – Now examine your horoscope by setting out the relevant Tarot cards in place of the astrological symbols. In other words, put the Sign cards in a circle and put the Planetary cards where indicated by your horoscope. Try to interpret the data purely on the basis of your Tarot knowledge. Record the results.

4 – Compare and contrast your two sets of results.

C ~ The Tree of Life: An Alternative Approach

I am indebted for this to the work of Mr. Michael Magee, whose article *A New Attribution*, published in SOTHIS magazine during the 1970's, opened new possibilities. Therein he argued persuasively that since the Tree of Life is just *a way* of structuring universal data, not the Universe Itself, there is nothing to prevent us from devising alternative means of ordering this data, providing that these structures have their internal logic and reveal truths.

Maps are a good analogy here. If we are in London and walking, driving or being driven, we will probably need an 'A–Z' street map which is precise in terms of locations and distances. But if we are travelling on the Underground, this will be of little use. We will need a London Transport map. This is wholly inaccurate in terms of scale of distances but we will need to know it, rather than the 'A–Z' if we are to travel successfully by tube.

The same is true of specialist guide-books. A brilliant exposition of how best to explore London's many exhibitions of culture and the arts is useless to the international gourmet who has come to town for the exclusive purpose of breakfasting, lunching and dining exquisitely; yet a work written specifically for the gourmet would drive the culture-vulture to Russian Roulette. Both works, however accurate, would do little to assist an international criminal keen on making contacts with the centres of organised crime: a rather differently structured guide-book would be required here. And William Blake's magnificent mapping of the sacred spots of London, while it delights and enchants the poet and mystic, could give the average tourist a nervous breakdown.

We need, then, different maps for different purposes. With the application of each map, we can learn more. However, we must not forget our original map of the Tree of Life any more than we should forget that, however the data is structured, Hampstead is north of Piccadilly.

That said, let us essay the exercise, which is based upon the Tree of Life but with the addition of the Sephirah briefly discussed in the previous chapter, Daath. For it is argued by many that we live in a New Aeon and that each New Aeon of human evolution requires a new system of classification of the Universe.

First place the 12 Sign cards in a circle from Aries to Pisces, to symbolise the stars beyond our solar system. Then, within this circle, lay out the cards as follows:–

1
Pluto
The Fool
Kether
The Crown

3
Neptune
The Universe
Binah
Understanding

2
Uranus
The Aeon
Chokmah
Wisdom

11
Saturn
The Hanged Man
Daath
Knowledge

5
Mars
The Tower
Geburah
Power

4
Jupiter
Fortune
Chesed
Glory

6
Sun
The Sun
Tiphareth
Beauty

8
Mercury
The Magus
Hod
Splendour

7
Venus
The Empress
Netzach
Victory

9
Moon
The Priestess
Yesod
Foundation

10
Earth
The Minor Arcana
Malkuth
Kingdom

Much knowledge of the nature of the Sephiroth and Planets can be derived by meditating upon this arrangement, yet it is open to criticism in its placement of the cards above 'The Abyss' — i.e. that gulf between Ideal and Actual which separates 1, 2, 3 and Daath from 4–10, that chasm between the consciousness of Man, however elevated, and the consciousness of the living Universe. Not for nothing is it stated that the aspiring mystic must, at a certain exalted stage of Adeptship, give up all that he has and all that he is in a marriage with the Universal Life which annihilates the ego.

Below the Abyss, Reason ends by contradicting itself, as the philosophical writings of Berkeley, Hume and Kant demonstrate all too clearly. Above the Abyss, all contradictions are resolved. We should not be unduly astonished, therefore, if the positioning of attributions above the Abyss has not yet been satisfactorily resolved. For there is a serious objection to the placings hitherto described.

How can Uranus at 2 be put before Neptune at 3 when everyone knows that Neptune is nearer than Uranus to Pluto at 1?

Other attributions above the Abyss have therefore been attempted.

	1	
	Pluto	
	The Fool	
3	Kether	2
Uranus		Neptune
The Aeon		The Hanged Man
Binah	11	Chokmah
	Saturn	
	The Universe	
	Daath	

This is even more open to criticism.

1 – Traditionally, 2, Chokmah, represents the Element Fire. How can we therefore attribute The Hanged Man, representing Water? Moreover, the Hebrew Letter Mem, which corresponds to The Hanged Man, means Water.

2 – Looking at Life and what we know of its behaviour, it is very difficult to accept that divine Wisdom resides in the self-sacrifice symbolised by The Hanged Man. The Trump could serve as a perfect glyph for the sacrifice of all that one has and is in crossing the Abyss from human to Divine, but it is hardly a satisfactory symbol for one who has attained beyond that and unto Wisdom.

3 – 3, Binah, is the sphere of receptive, feminine Understanding. What is the fiery and disruptive planet Uranus doing there? And how can Binah, the Great Mother, be reconciled with a symbol so expressive of masculine energy as The Aeon, even in its older form of Judgement?

4 – Such knowledge as we have associates Uranus with Magic and Neptune with Mysticism, a doctrine beautifully reflected in *Symphony of the Planets* by Gustav Holst. Therefore Neptune appears to have much in common with Binah and Uranus with Chokmah. Yet how can this be reconciled with their positions in the solar system?

We can probably learn something from the above endeavour but ultimately, it simply will not do. Let us examine Crowley's proposal.

		1		
		Pluto		
		The Fool		
3		Kether		2
Saturn				Neptune
The Universe				The Hanged Man
Binah		11		Chokmah
		Uranus		
		The Aeon		
		Daath		

This is still open to all the objections relating to the Chokmah — Hanged Man problem as outlined above. I have proposed another one.

38

1
Pluto
The Fool
Kether

3
Saturn
The Universe
Binah

11
Neptune
The Hanged Man
Daath

2
Uranus
The Aeon
Chokmah

This does not violate any of the canons of traditional Qabalistic doctrine. The violation is in terms of Astronomy. One still has to justify putting Neptune 'below' Uranus and Saturn. Three reasons can be stated.

A – Daath connects directly with Kether.

B – Daath is not in a set of two dimensional lines but at a three dimensional angle to Kether, Chokmah and Binah.

C – Neptune the Mystic is appropriately placed for the experience known as Crossing the Abyss.

Are these arguments really convincing? The student should examine the data and make up his own mind, for the matter remains in a state of flux, like the Universe Itself. Perhaps one could try forgetting Daath altogether as not being a Sephirah at all, an argument sanctioned by qabalistic tradition. This could possibly lead to a more coherent arrangement.

At this point, some readers may have lost all patience and find themselves unable to see the point at all. Why juggle with the cards and their meanings?

For the same reason that mathematicians and physicists juggle with equations and chemists constantly experiment: to try and order the data Life presents to us so as to make sense of it. Man is a pattern-making animal.

Nor should we forget that Binary Mathematics, which was created by Leibniz as a work of 'pointless juggling with figures' and seemed to have no practical application, is what made the computer possible.

In the traditional Tarot decks, The Magus is called The Juggler. The Magus corresponds with Mercury, Planet and Roman God, and with the Egyptian equivalent Thoth, God of Magick, the Word and Wisdom. Not for nothing did Crowley call the Tarot The Book of Thoth.

As if this whole matter of attribution were not complex and controversial enough, I was recently informed by Mr. Roy Alexander, the noted astrologer, that one school of thought attributes Pluto/The Fool to Daath and Neptune/The Hanged Man to Kether (Uranus/The Aeon is in Chokmah and Saturn/The Universe in Binah); here, one asks what The Hanged Man, symbol of the Dying God, the Piscean Age and the Old Aeon is doing in Kether. And if all things come from the Void symbolised by The Fool, what is he doing in Daath?

There doesn't appear to be an attribution which satisfies all the data and is above reproach. Tentatively, I would propose a possible way out of this dilemma. It is that all the equations so far proposed have a certain validity. I would suggest that above the Abyss — that is, Kether, Chokmah, Binah and Daath — energy behaves as it does within the atom, in the manner described by quantum theory. Just as electrons abruptly change their positions without appearing to travel any intervening distance in quantum 'jumps', so the energies above the Abyss are in a constant state of flux and interchange. No map can therefore be absolutely right, for we cannot fix what is in flux. However, any given map might describe accurately a given instant in time.

Any given map which has its own coherent logic can prove very useful and for some purposes, indispensable. One judges by the results of applying it.

In order first to apprehend and then to do something useful with the information at our disposal, it is essential to undertake experiments and then to find satisfying coherent ways of arranging our knowledge. This will enable us to classify conveniently all data at our disposal, which in turn will enable us to explore new areas from established points of reference. One purpose of this chapter has been to show the students how investigations into the esoteric are conducted by its pioneers. As Crowley stated, we do indeed study Tarot with 'the Aim of Religion': but the means consist of 'The Method of Science'.

There remains much more to explore. Let us turn to Mythology.

CHAPTER 5

Mythology

Mythology, legend and folk-lore are probably the most genuine expression of that which any people feels to be true of the nature of Life and of itself. This makes for wonderful stories which still inspire creative artists — and audiences undebauched by the valium of too much television. Although humanity has had experience of many varying geographical and climatic conditions, prompting many different ethical beliefs, we all share the same fundamental myths on the global village which our planet has become. The essential identity of these myths led Carl Jung to posit the existence of the Collective Unconscious, something far deeper than the personal subconscious, a great and virtually ageless mind shared in common by each and every member of humanity, past, present and future, which manifests in myth, legend, folk-lore and dream.

Fundamental to this notion is the idea of *archetypes*. These are powerful symbols which appear in universal myths and dreams: they are symbols of great force; and they lead us to greater understanding of ourselves, to the goal Jung termed *individuation*: which is self-understanding and the perfect harmonising of all our faculties, enabling us to rejoice in Life and in a fruitful and fulfilling relationship with the Universe.

Jung was not alone among psychologists in perceiving the central importance of Mythology to an understanding of the human mind. His one-time teacher, Sigmund Freud, discerned profound significance in, for instance, the Greek myth of Oedipus. Here, although Oedipus is a hero who solves the Riddle of the Sphinx which is the Riddle of Man; as prophesied he unknowingly slays his father and marries his mother; this brings drought to his kingdom; and when the nature of his actions is brought home to him by the blind seer Tiresias, he is so horrified that he abdicates and puts out his eyes with the needles of his mother's jewels. Freud held that this tale embodied a universal truth of Man: that all males subconsciously want to kill their fathers and make love to their mothers, which forbidden actions cause repression, guilt, the 'sin complex' and in some cases, psychological devastation. The Oedipus complex has also been held responsible for homosexuality and sado-masochism.

The study of mythology is consequently not merely the innocent enjoyment of tales told by our ancestors; it is the study of the structure of our minds. Naturally the Tarot reflects this. One of its many functions is as an encyclopedia of universal myths.

In order to appreciate this chapter fully, the reader will require a sound, basic knowledge of mythology, to be acquired before or after its perusal. One can safely recommend *The Greek Myths* and *The White Goddess* by Robert Graves or the *Larousse Encyclopedia of Mythology*, which are invaluable: but Mythology is best enjoyed and appreciated in one or several of the many excellent books put out for children, especially those illustrated by fine artists. No reader can afford to neglect the joys inherent in these; and the same is true of any serious student.

Most students of the Tarot want to know what the cards mean and this is a natural and legitimate request. But it is rather like asking: 'What does the colour "red" mean?' One cannot define any Tarot card in the precise sense that we can define a word by the dictionary. What we can do is indicate its parameters. So far, basic divinatory meanings, qabalistic meanings and astrological meanings have been given. It is for the student to integrate all this information into that private Temple of Wisdom each one of us must build for ourselves. Mythology provides us with a quarry of rich materials.

The subject is not without its difficulties even although we have our splendid tool of classification in the Tree of Life. However, let us take an example in the Egyptian Goddess Isis. As Crowley remarks in 777:

'...Isis might be given to Zero as conterminous with Nature, to 3 as Mother, to 4 as Venus to 6 as Harmony, to 7 as Love, to 9 as the Moon, to 10 as Virgin, to 13 again as the Moon, to

14 as Venus, to 15 as connected with the letter Heh, to 16 as the Sacred Cow, to 18 as Goddess of Water, to 24 as Draco, to 28 as Giver of Rain, to 29 as the Moon, and to 32 as Lady of the Mysteries (Saturn, Binah).'

And, one might add, to 2 as Wisdom.

All this is actually less confusing than it appears to be. For Isis is a multi-faceted deity, worshipped by humanity in divers circumstances and therefore in divers forms over many centuries. Analysis through the Tree of Life enables us to perceive the many ideas summarised in the concept — or energy aggregate — of Isis. However, we will not find notions of the Sun or Mars, for instance. But we must bear in mind the elasticity of mythological conceptions. They merge into one another rather like the way in which things do in dreams, though the scope of each conception other than 0, however broad, is ultimately limited.

Given this, let us explore some of the mythological correspondences of the Tarot Trumps. Volumes could be written on the subject but space is limited and I trust that the reader will forgive what is merely a brief exposition of essentials.

0 The Fool is Nothing and therefore All. From the union of male and female within the androgynous Fool, all created things proceed. He is the supreme form of Pan, which word means 'All'.

The Fool is divine ecstasy, that rapture of union with the Universe which makes everything else meaningless by comparison and which is yet termed foolishness by the worldly wise. His wisdom is earthly folly and his folly is heavenly wisdom. We find this in all legends which pertain to 'holy men' who speak the will of the Gods but whom many find indistinguishable from village idiots.

He embodies the eruptions of Spring. He is the unconscious impulse exploding within us, eager to embrace each and every experience in an ecstatic spasm of love for creation. He is Parzival, and the Knight Errant of Fairy Tales, whose innocence, though reviled by men, enables him to redeem the Earth. In German fairy stories, he is the innocent peasant who marries the King's daughter and ascends to the throne. In Middle Eastern legends, he is the Mullah Nasrudin.

In Egyptian mythology, The Fool is Hoor-paar-kraat (Harpocrates), the silent Babe in the Egg from whom all things proceed and return. In Graeco-Roman mythology, he is Zeus Arrhenothelus, the All-Begetter, and Dionysus and Bacchus, the intoxicated Redeemer of Mankind. In Christianity, being Air, he is the Holy Ghost. In all religions, he is the Creative Light.

It is interesting to observe the debased medieval continuation of the Fool in a secular context. At the courts of kings, only one functionary was allowed to depart from servile and sycophantic flattery of the monarch and tell the truth, though this was done in the form of jest. This functionary was the court Fool. His comedy and his tragedy have been unforgettably portrayed by Shakespeare in *King Lear*.

Crowley has also left us with haunting remarks on The Fool in *The Wake World*.

'Last of all is the most mysterious passage of them all, and if any of you saw it you would think there was a foolish man in it being bitten by crocodiles and dogs, and carrying a sack with nothing any use at all in it. But really it is the man who meant to wake up, and did wake up. So that is his House, he is the old King himself, and so are you. So he wouldn't care what any one thought he was.'

(Konx Om Pax)

The Fool survives in our modern pack of playing cards as The Joker.

I *The Magus*: in traditional packs he is termed The Juggler and depicted with wand, cup, sword and disk, which represent Will, Love, Mind and Body and are the weapons of the practising Magician. The Fool is the divine Will and the Magus is the Word which gives expression to it.

It should not surprise us to discover that during the hundreds of years during which truth was obscured by the murky clouds of dogmatic Christianity backed up by well-organised bodies of torturers, that the divine Word was pictured as a vulgar street trickster. But there is a deeper metaphysical truth herein. At his highest, The Magus represents Thoth, the Egyptian God of Wisdom, Magick, Writing and the Word. On the Tree of Life, this equates with 2, Chokmah, Wisdom, and with the Path between 3, Binah, Understanding and 1, Kether, The Crown. However, in Egyptian mythology, Thoth is usually accompanied by an ape-like creature who mocks the God's words. This Ape is to be found in Hindu mythology as Hanuman, the cunning and mischievous Monkey-God, who equates with 8, Hod, the sphere of mundane intellect. This shows that the finite brains of human beings are usually incapable of apprehending divine wisdom. It is spoken but not understood and so is debased.

Even in daily life we are familiar with how even the simplest statements, when repeated, can become altered out of all recognition. Bill might say: 'I've got a bulldog' and this can go through the processes of: 'Bill's got a bull-terrier'; 'Bill's got a fox-terrier.' 'Bill's got a foxhound'; 'Bill's got a greyhound'; 'Bill's got a grey dog'; 'Bill's dog is nearly black'; 'Bill's dog is dirty'; and finally, 'They say you're a dirty dog, Bill.'

In the same way, Truths intended to liberate Mankind become twisted out of all recognition and end as engines of tyranny.

The corresponding Gods in Greek and Roman mythology are Hermes and Mercury, who at their highest equate with 2, Chokmah, and at their lowest with 8, Hod. To pass from Chokmah to Hod is to cross the Abyss from Ideal to Actual and to find Wisdom degenerating into intellectualism and being street-smart.

The Magus is Mercurius, the unifying symbol. At his highest, he is the Messenger of the Gods and supreme creative artist. At his lowest in 8, he is not only the God of human reason and writing, but of merchants, liars, tricksters, doctors, accountants, lawyers and thieves.

The Magus is also Prometheus who steals the fire from Heaven and gives it to men.

And in all mythologies, he is the Trickster. Loki in Norse mythology is one example, but perhaps the most exalted conception here is in Buddhism, where he is Mayan, the Great Sorcerer who has made this Universe, which is just an illusion.

II *The Priestess:* she is Isis, especially as Eternal Virgin and Lady of the Mysteries. She is the White Goddess, the Muse of the poets, Virgin who gives to all who ask yet who remains intact.

She is Artemis and Diana, virgin huntresses and Goddesses of the Moon, in its purest and most exalted conception. Her Divine Light is the Veil of True Spirit. She is the pure, eternal feminine.

In Magick, she is the Holy Guardian Angel to whom one aspires and who in the End awaits one above the Abyss.

III The Empress: she is Woman as Real rather than as Ideal. Her function is that of the Wife. The Priestess arouses Man to aspire; The Empress enables him to earth it.

She is Goddess of Love; Hathor in Egypt, Aphrodite in Greece, Venus in Rome.

As consort of The Emperor, she equates with the Queen Goddesses, the Greek Hera and the Roman Juno.

As Demeter, she is Nature, and not only its bounty and fruitfulness, but 'Nature red in tooth and claw.'

IV The Emperor: he is the Mighty Ruler who governs all with his orb and his crown and his sceptre; the Greek Zeus, the Roman Jupiter, the Norse Odin, the Teutonic Wotan, the Hindu Indra. On Earth he is the archetype of the great warrior-kings such as Arthur, Charlemagne and Alexander.

The swift, creative and masculine energy of The Emperor reinforces the idea of the warrior. Hence he is also the Greek Ares and the Roman Mars, Gods of War; and Yahweh, Lord of Hosts.

However, as the Ruler who conserves the kingdom, he is an aspect of Vishnu the Preserver in Hinduism.

As The Empress symbolises Woman, so The Emperor is Man.

V The Hierophant: he used to be called the Pope and is High Priest of the Sacred Mysteries. He is Osiris as Initiator, Asar the Redeemer.

There is the Taurus connection of The Hierophant and the Bull. Here he is Apis the Redeemer and in Hinduism, Shiva as Lord of the Mysteries. He equates with the Norse Odin as the Supreme Wise One.

As Crowley realised in his design, there is a feminine aspect to this card. She is best represented by Pallas Athena, warrior Goddess of Wisdom, who sprang fully armed from the head of Zeus.

The Hierophant heralds each succeeding stage of human evolution.

VI The Lovers: portrayed in the traditional design by a man trying to choose between two women with Cupid poised in the air above him. Thus this card obviously pertains to Eros/Cupid whose arrows of love slay all reason in pursuit of its rapture.

Superficial commentators held that one woman was Bad and the other was Good, which showed that Man Must Make The Right Choice — but the Tarot hardly stands for anything quite so dismally platitudinous. Crowley caught the traditional spirit more accurately:

'The passage where the twins live is very difficult too. They are two sisters; and one is very pure and good, and the other is a horrid fast woman. But that shows you how silly dream language is — really there is another way to put it: you can say they are two sisters, and one is very silly and ignorant, and the other has learnt to know and enjoy.

'Now when one is a Princess it is very important to have good manners; so you have to go into the passage, and take one on each arm, and go through with them singing and dancing; and if you hurt the feelings of either of them the least little bit in the world it would show you were not really a great lady, only a dress lady, and there is a man with a bow and arrow in the air, and he would soon finish you, and you would never get to the Third House at all.'

(*The Wake World* from Konx Om Pax)

The Crowley-Harris design goes further in terms of symbolism too. Two lovers are shown uniting in mystic marriage, blessed by a hooded figure representing IX The Hermit, though Cupid also appears. The Lovers is quintessentially a card of Alchemy in its portrayal of the union of opposites.

In terms of Tetragrammaton, the Lovers are the Son and the Daughter of The Father and The Mother and so Twins, appropriate in view of the astrological attribution of Gemini. The card therefore refers also to all twin deities such as Castor and Pollux.

In its most material form, it recalls all the great love stories of the world.

VII The Chariot: this recalls Apollo the Charioteer, whose vehicle bears the Sun. But a more satisfying alternative is the view that the Charioteer bears the Holy Graal.

The beasts which draw the Chariot are referred to the Sphinx and are portrayed as sphinxes in the Crowley-Harris deck.

The Sphinx is the guardian of the Riddle of Man and embodies the Four Powers of Magick: To Know, to Dare, to Will and to Be Silent.

VIII Adjustment: this card is often termed Justice. But there is no justice as we know it in the Universe. There is exactitude and the precise rectification of imbalance. One might well refer it to the Greek Nemesis, the automatic justice of Nature.

Adjustment also corresponds to the Goddesses of justice, the Greek Themis and especially, the Egyptian Maat.

She is Karma, the Law of Cause and Effect. 'As ye sow, so shall ye reap.' 'Those who live by the sword, shall perish by the sword.' 'All you do will return to you.'

In Alchemy, Adjustment is the Woman Justified.

IX The Hermit: he obviously encapsulates all the legends of wise, old men. Merlin springs to mind.

There is a sense too in which, as pure, phallic force equating with Yod, the All-Father, The Hermit is supreme.

'Then there was a really lovely passage, like a deep wood in Springtime, the dearest old man came along who had lived there all his life, because he was the guardian of it, and he didn't need to travel because he belonged to the First House really from the very beginning. He wore a vast cloak, and he carried a lamp and a long stick; and he said that the cloak meant you were to be silent and not say anything you saw, and the lamp meant you were to tell everybody and make them glad, and the stick was like a guide to tell you which to do. But I didn't quite believe that, because I am getting a grown-up girl now, and I wasn't to be put off like that. I could see that the stick was really the measuring rod with which the whole Palace was built, and the lamp was the only light they had to build it by, and the cloak was the abyss of darkness that covers it all up.'

(Crowley: *The Wake World* from *Konx Om Pax*)

X Fortune: the correspondences with Jupiter obviously suggest that God or his Greek form of Zeus in his most abstract form. Brahma the Creator would be the Hindu and Amoun-Ra the Egyptian equivalents.

The three figures on the wheel can be read as primary Fire, Air and Water through which the All-Father manifests. Other parallels are the Three Fates of Western Mythology; and in Hinduism, the three Gunas — Sattvas, Rajas and Tamas — out of which all things are composed. They are also the Sulphur, Mercury and Salt of Alchemy.

In the Crowley-Harris deck, they are portrayed as the Sphinx at the top, with Hermanubis, the creative form of Mercury ascending, and Typhon, deity of destruction, descending.

The Wheel is that of existence, of birth, life, death and reincarnation.

XI: *Lust:* this is called so to emphasise not just strength, as of yore, but joy of strength exercised. In the traditional packs, the woman represents the Egyptian lioness-headed Goddess Sekhmet and/or her equally fierce Hindu equivalent, Durga.

In the few packs where a man is shown with a Lion, this stands for legends of encounters between Man and Beast such as Samson's slaying of the lion and his saying: 'Out of the strong came forth sweetness; Hercules' conquest of the lion; and Daniel in the lions' den.

The woman and the lion stand for the many legends of union between the human female and a God in the form of a beast: e.g. Leda and the Swan.

Myth has it that the result of such unions is a divine or semi-divine being: e.g. Hermes or Dionysus.

In the Bible, we have the Beast and the Scarlet Woman of *Revelations.* Crowley proudly portrayed them in his recension of the card. For him, there were no evil connotations, just the ecstasy of union between male and female, God and Goddess from which flow all created things. The Beast is God, Man and Animal conjoined; the Woman is Babalon the Great Goddess and she bears the Holy Graal.

XII: *The Hanged Man:* he represents those Gods who sacrifice themselves to redeem humanity — Asar, Adonis, Attis, Osiris and of course, Jesus Christ. They are Dying Gods — but they rise again.

He is also Odin the Shaman, who hanged himself upside down from a sacred tree in order to acquire his powers.

Because Mem, the corresponding Hebrew letter, means water, he corresponds with the sea Gods, Poseidon and Neptune.

He can also be taken to represent the Oedipus complex, which Freud thought to be the root of guilt and sin complexes generally.

XIII Death: this card obviously stands for death.

A further association is Saturn as Father Time.

XIV Art: the figure represents Nepthys, the Black Isis in Egyptian Mythology. In Graeco-Roman mythology, and partly on account of the Sagittarius association, she is Diana the Huntress.

In Hinduism, she is Kali, who creates from and reduces all to putrefaction.

However, the primary significance of Art is Alchemical. It portrays the result of the Mystic Marriage of VI The Lovers.

XV The Devil: he represents Pan, the All-Begetter, Set in Egyptian Mythology, and Baphomet, the idol allegedly worshipped by the Knights Templar. All phallic deities such as Priapus and Bacchus can be attributed to The Devil.

To impose a Christian perspective is to misunderstand the nature of the card, which is the blind, instinctive and irrepressible force of Nature.

XVI The Tower: this card reminds one of the fall of Jericho; but it is also a glyph of the impact of the divine on human consciousness. All preconceptions are shattered. In Hinduism there is the doctrine of the Eye of Shiva, which, when opened, destroys the Universe. A similar power is attributed to the Egyptian God, Horus.

Horus is, among other things, the God of War and so this card is also associated with the Greek Ares and the Roman Mars.

XVII The Star: this portrays Nuit, the Supreme Goddess of the stars. She is also the Great Mother in whose womb we are all begotten.

XVIII The Moon: this is the waning moon of witchcraft and sacred to Hecate. Herein is glamour, illusion, fantasy and sorcery.

The dogs, wolves and/or jackals in the card represent Anubis, the Egyptian jackal-headed God, who guides the soul through the Underworld.

50

The crab-like creature in traditional packs is more properly the Midnight Beetle, Kheph-Ra in Egyptian mythology, who bears the sacred bark of the Sun in its nightly journey through the darkness.

XIX The Sun: all Sun Gods are represented here — the Graeco-Roman Helios and Apollo, the Egyptian Ra etc.

The child or children represent that complete freedom towards which humanity is painfully evolving.

XX The Aeon: this used to be called Judgement and in it an Angel awoke the dead with the blast of the Last Trump. The Christian symbolism is obvious.

Gods of Judgement and of Fire are represented here: the Hindu Agni (Fire) and Yama (Judgement), the Greek Hades, the Roman Pluto and the Egyptian Horus.

In the Crowley-Harris deck, the symbolism has been altered in the light of *The Book of the Law* to symbolise a New Aeon for humanity. Infinite Space and unlimited possibility are shown by the Goddess Nuit; the force within the atom, the infinitely small Point which is everywhere, is shown by the winged globe, the God Hadit. All things come from the perpetual mating of Nuit and Hadit. According to *The Book of the Law*, their most important conjunction from the point of view of our planet is the God Heru-Ra-Ha, Lord or Ruling Force of the Earth during the next evolutionary stage.

Heru-Ra-Ha is a form of Horus and a double-god. In his active form, he is the hawk-headed Ra-Hoor-Khuit; in his passive form, he is the silent Hoor-paar-kraat, the Babe in the Egg.

XXI The Universe: the woman is The Daughter of Tetragrammaton. She is Mother Earth, Ceres the Corn Goddess, Persephone in profusion of manifestation.

The Four Beasts around her represent the Four Elements and the Four Powers of the Sphinx.

Nothing has manifested as Creative Light in The Fool and gone through twenty stages to manifest as Everything in The Universe, which will itself return to Nothing and The Fool.

I hope that the reader has found this listing of associations and allusions to be helpful. As will readily have been seen, some

51

cards are much more complex than others — and only the principal correspondences have been delineated. The interested reader is best advised to soak himself in Mythology on the basis of the above, for this will greatly increase appreciation of the Tarot. One glance at a glyph will evoke a stream of suggestive thoughts. It is an interesting exercise to contemplate a particular card while allowing all legends connected with it to flow through the mind.

This requires some words on Meditation.

NOTE

The subject of Tarot, myth and legend has been explored brilliantly in the novel The Castle of Crossed Destinies by Italo Calvino. Here the Tarot is laid out in patterns from which twenty-four archetypal tales are derived. The work ranks among the finest examples of creative use of the cards.

CHAPTER 6

Meditation

How is the data on the Tarot to be profitably assimilated? The best method is popularly termed meditation. Set aside a certain time of the day and use it to contemplate each card in turn. This is a process which must be gone through time and time again, for the keys take on new meaning with each succeeding session.

Note every detail of symbolism and ask yourself why it is there. What precise effect do the colours have on you? Afterwards, record everything you did not understand and try to solve the problem by using works of reference. Bring your discoveries to the next stage.

Let all the information you have on the card in question flow through the mind. Try to perceive connections between these ideas, above all, the central concept which links all of them. Then proceed from the known to the unknown. Quietly observe which thoughts arise spontaneously in your mind when a particular card is before you.

If you have been or are a compulsive collector of Tarot packs, as the present writer was for a period, you can now do something useful with even the most futile of decks. Lay out the various versions of a particular card and see what they have in common.

Always keep a record and read through it at least every three months.

The foregoing exercises are warmly recommended but strictly speaking, they are not *meditation* at all, contrary to all the nonsense that has been written and spoken on the subject. Then what should one call them? 'Quiet observation' and 'Creative imagination' seem to describe accurately the mental processes involved. Although these are essential preliminaries for most, in too many cases they degenerate into sterile reverie and idle day-dream.

For meditation is the one-pointed restraining of the mind to a single word, sound, image or thought. The best results come from arduous and at times excruciating concentration.

The method is to focus your entire attention upon the card chosen without permitting any distraction whatsoever to enter the mind. Although this process may even seem pleasant at first, it soon becomes torment. In order to record your progress, you make a mark on a piece of paper every time your attention wanders in any way from the card. The itches, twitches and aches of your body will be a prime source of interference and this problem is best solved by taking up Yoga — but the body is only the beginning. There is no limit to the monkey-tricks the mind can play. Memories, dreams, reflections, ruminations, even snatches of songs and other irrelevant intrusions will rape your attention time and time again.

A great threat to your fixity of thought will in fact be the knowledge of the Tarot which you have painfully learned but which will disturb the mind you are trying to keep perfectly still and quiet and concentrated entirely upon a visual image. You may also suffer from an inner critical commentary on your meditation. A voice within you says: 'I'm doing well,' or 'Total concentration at last!' Unfortunately, you will also find that as your awareness of your mind and vigilance over it increase, your powers of concentration will seem to be getting worse and worse.

Take comfort. If after 28 days of 5 minutes a day, you can go 93 seconds without a break in thought, you are making good progress. 31 seconds would be satisfactory. Sadly, most do not finish the course. The advantages of this method are:

1 – It is the supreme way of training the mind.
2 – It is the most direct way of opening the hidden depths of the mind, and of opening it to the hidden depths of the Tarot.
3 – If pursued diligently it leads to the summits of mystical experience.

Meditation, Quiet Observation and Creative Imagination should always be practised with a straight spine, a posture which is steady and easy and breathing that is easy, deep, regular and slow.

I have kept this chapter short quite deliberately for there is nothing more to add other than Crowley's key words:

'Sit still.
Stop thinking.
Shut up.
Get out.'

CHAPTER 7

Morality, Medicine and More Methods

Most writers agree that the Tarot embodies a secret doctrine of Wisdom. This is perfectly true. The secrecy lies not in the power of any sinister society but in the difficulty of trying to expound in words that which is beyond them. One could broadcast the secrets on world-wide television and few would be one whit the wiser.

Ludwig Wittgenstein, arguably the twentieth century's greatest Western philosopher, concluded in his *Tractatus Logico-Philosophicus* that only two sorts of proposition have meaning: those which state that something is the same as something else, like definitions or the propositions of mathematics: and those which can be tested by experiment, like the propositions of science. He held in the *Tractatus* that strictly speaking, all other propositions lack logic and make no sense at all. Yet, as he continued:

'There is indeed the mystical. This shows itself.'

An advantage of the Tarot is that it can show what words cannot adequately describe. Words on the Tarot certainly have their indispensable use as guides but one is ultimately reminded of the Zen proverb: 'Teaching is like pointing a finger at the Moon. The student must look at the Moon and not at the finger.'

Questions of Morality enter into most books on the Tarot. There is a regrettable tendency on the part of many authors to use the cards as a vehicle for their own painfully limited notions. One reads all too often, for instance, that XV The Devil just symbolises bondage to fleshly lusts and materialism which is A Bad Thing. Sections on VIII Adjustment (Justice) often teach us that it is good to be Good and bad to be Bad. XX The Aeon (Judgement) has been used to inform us that the wicked will be punished and the good rewarded — comforting, no doubt, to the multi-million victims of war, genocide, famine, torture and pestilence.

This trivialisation of the Tarot is intensely irritating. It is as though the Powers of the Universe were expected to conform to the mores of some exceptionally dull, lower middle class, provincial suburb. Small wonder that Crowley felt moved to parody this Sunday School attitude in his remarks on XIV Art in *The Wake World*.

'Then there was another passage called the Arrow by Day, and there was a most lovely lady all shining with the sun, and moon, and stars, who was lighting a great bowl of water with one hand, by dropping dew on it out of a cup, and with the other she was putting out a terrible fire with a torch. She had a red lion and a white eagle, that she had always had ever since she was a little girl. She had found them in a nasty pit full of all kinds of filth, and they were very savage; but by always treating them kindly they had grown up faithful and good. This should be a lesson to all of us never to be unkind to our pets.'

(Konx Om Pax.)

The Tarot can assist us to lead a more fulfilling life but only if we understand its function. Tarot keys are no more 'moral' or 'immoral' than the Law of Gravity or the Law of Inverse Squares, which Laws we can use to benefit ourselves. For each one of you is here on Earth to know and be yourself — the divine essence within you; just as water should seek its level, sheep should eat grass and wolves should eat sheep. The Tarot is in accord with the Law of Nature. Provided we realise this, the keys will serve as astute guides to a more liberated and enlightened life.

To begin with, contemplation of the Aces can bring out Will, Understanding, Mind and Material Effectiveness from within us. The cards numbered 2–10 in the Minor Arcana analyse situations described by the titles, showing how these can be brought about.

'The 6 of Wands is referred to Jupiter in Leo, and called the Lord of Victory. This indicates not only what victory is like, but also the conditions to be fulfilled in order to obtain victory. There is need of the fiery energy of the suit of Wands, the balance of the Number 6, the stubborn courage of Leo and also the influence of Jupiter, the little bit of luck that tips the scales.'

(Crowley: *The Book of Thoth*.)

This formula can (and should) be applied to every card. In times of failure, for instance, one should study Failure, the 7 of Disks, to discern how the factors which make up the card apply to one's own position. The way out of failure is to apply the opposite qualities.

The Court Cards can be used for psychological analysis. Take the key which represents you and examine which aspects of your own life cause your best qualities to degenerate into your worst. The Court Cards are also useful aids to working out relationships. Whenever you are thinking on a problem here, have before you the cards which best represent the person(s) involved. Endeavour to perceive what matters of friction might obtain between the cards and apply that to the situation in question.

The Trumps can be used to rectify imbalances in your own psyche. Persistent attention to the appropriate key can enhance a quality you lack or alleviate a harmful excess. Here is a simple table:–

Trump		*Enhances*	*Alleviates*
0	The Fool	Joy; creativity; laughter	Repression.
I	The Magus	Clear thought; elasticity	Rigidity of mind/ behaviour.
II	The Priestess	Inspiration; intuition.	Over-intellectualism.
III	The Empress	Harmony; generosity.	Meanness
IV	The Emperor	Courage.	Cowardice.
V	The Hierophant	Spiritual progress.	Anxiety.
VI	The Lovers	Love.	Anger.
VII	The Chariot	Single-mindedness.	Vacillation.
VIII	Adjustment	Equilibrium	Mental chaos.
IX	The Hermit	Self-sufficiency.	Social insecurity.
X	Fortune	Life-acceptance.	Life-denial.
XI	Lust	Strength	Weakness
XII	Hanged Man	Endurance.	Resentment.
XIII	Death	Perception.	Depression.
XIV	Art	Understanding	Confusion.
XV	The Devil	Will; instinct.	Guilt.
XVI	The Tower	Energy.	Egotism.
XVII	The Star	Rapture.	Envy.
XVIII	The Moon	Imagination.	Dullness
XIX	The Sun	Spontanaeity	Frustration.
XX	The Aeon	Drive	Sloth
XXI	The Universe	Gladness	Boredom.

It is merely a matter of choosing the relevant card to be your doctor and giving it frequent consultation. Quiet observation will do, though strict meditation is the best means. Those who work with this method and so encounter the keys as healers will soon enough agree with the present writer's description of the Tarot as a 'guide, philosopher and friend.'

Before we tackle more theory, here are more ways of getting to know the Tarot even better. They consist of laying out various arrangements and trying to perceive both the individuality of each card and the pattern to which each card is contributing.

1 – Lay out each suit from Ace to Ten and regard the various transformations of the original Elemental Energy.

2 – Lay out each set of Court Cards in turn and think of Tetragrammaton. See the Knight as the Father, the original, magical Will; the Queen as the Mother, the mystical acceptance which is Understanding; the Prince as the Alchemical Son, born of their union; and the Daughter as the final, material result. Then remember that the Son will set the Daughter on the Throne of the Mother for the process to commence again, like a whirling wheel. Such is the transformation from Energy to Matter and back again.

3 – Contemplate the Four Knights together. Repeat with the Four Queens, Princes and Princesses in turn. Where are they similar and where do they differ?

4 – Examine the Minor Arcana in sets of four from the Aces to the Tens with the same attitude.

5 – Separate, in the way you think best, the male Trumps, the female Trumps and the Trumps which are both male and female. Scrutinise each of the three sets. Record your observations.

6 – Try the following patterns of 3

		Suggestive Summary
i –	The Fool - The Magus - The Hermit.	Manifestation of God.
ii –	The Priestess - The Empress - The Star.	Manifestation of Goddess

iii –	Fortune - The Emperor - The Hierophant	Masculine Energy.
iv –	Lust - Art - Adjustment.	Feminine Energy.
v –	The Lovers - Lust - Art.	Alchemy; divine and human mingled to effect Change.
vi –	The Moon - The Sun - The Aeon	Evolutionary progress.
vii –	The Devil - Art - Death	Gateways to individual superconsciousness. Annihilation of ego.
viii –	The Hanged Man - The Tower - The Chariot.	
ix –	The Lovers - The Priestess - The Star.	Gateways to cosmic superconsciousness.
x –	The Priestess - The Sun - The Fool.	The Supreme Initiation.
xi –	The Fool - Adjustment - The Universe	Whole course of the Tarot and Life.

Devise other Triads of your own.

7 – Lay the cards down one by one, from 0 to XXI to illustrate a story you make up and tell to an interested friend or to yourself. Try several stories. Experiment, if you wish, with the genres of fairy tale, science fiction, fantasy, crime, history, romance and thriller.

These methods all lead to an essential point. Through a thorough integration of the Tarot with its every resonance in the psyche, we too can thrill to its divine dance and embrace its living forces as we would willing partners.

CHAPTER 8

Tarot and I-Ching

The Eastern counterpart of the Tarot is the I-Ching or *Book of Changes* which originated over three thousand years ago in China, the world's oldest continuous civilisation. The I-Ching derives from the philosophy of Taoism as expounded in the *Tao Teh Ching*.

Tao cannot be declared either by speech or by silence. It is beyond both. No attempt to express its nature can possibly succeed, for it is beyond all human comprehension. It is beyond even Alpha and Omega, the First and the Last. The *Tao Teh Ching* states that we should have union with this Tao we cannot express. If we have union with this inexpressible, inconceivable, incomprehensible Tao, all is as it should be.

Teh is how Tao manifests itself in the Universe: and the Chinese sages created a symbol to express Tao Teh — the Yin-Yang. This consists of a circle equally divided by a serpentine curve into black and white portions. The black portion (Yin) and the white portion (Yang) together express the nature of the Universe in action. There is continuous interplay between them. Yang is, for instance, male, fire, positive, dominant and Yin is female, water, negative, yielding; and the constant interplay between Yin and Yang is the nature of all. Yang and Yin are the pairs of opposites into which all phenomena can be divided.

What needs to be stressed about the Yin-Yang symbol is that it is not a *rigid* division into pairs of opposites: the Chinese perceive these opposites as flowing into one another in a constant interchange of energies. This is why there is the white spot of Yang at the centre of Yin and the black spot of Yin at the centre of Yang. Once one has grasped the nature of this symbol, it becomes easier to understand the *Tao Teh*

Ching. It recommends that one should become aware of the Yin-Yang within oneself and in the Universe, balance the Yin and Yang within and without oneself and go with it, flow with it as if one were water seeking its level. This is why the Way of the Tao has been described as 'the art of doing everything by doing nothing.'

The *Tao Teh Ching* begins with aphorisms or 'strands of thought' which point to how one may become one with, and so — Tao. It goes on to recommend practical courses of conduct in a wide variety of situations — Teh. One who is in accordance with Tao will manifest Teh in all matters, great and small, from the governance of a kingdom to 'the nice conduct of a clouded cane'. For he will have Yin and Yang in perfect balance, and Yin and Yang will manifest, not *by* the self but *through* the self. This endeavour to express the inexpressible is obviously inadequate. One can only exhort the reader to turn to the original work.

Essentially, the I-Ching is applied Taoism. It is said that Confucius declared that had he another fifty years to live, he would devote each day of each year to study of the I-Ching. This begins with Tao Teh in the form of the Yin-Yang. Then Yin is symbolised by a broken line ━ ━, and Yang by a straight line ━. Yin and Yang, the broken line and the straight line, are how Tao Teh manifests. The Chinese sages proceeded to construct a system based on Yin-Yang interaction: 8 'trigrams', the 8 possible ways of putting together 3 lines from the straight and the broken. Since these 8 symbols were insufficiently complex to render a detailed understanding of universal phenomena, they multiplied the system into 64 symbols, created through combining the original 8 trigrams with the same 8 trigrams in combinations of 6 lines, which they called 'hexagrams'. In other words, there are 64 possible ways of combining a straight line and a broken line in symbols of 6 lines. This is the basis of the I-Ching.

If one wishes to consult the I-Ching, one asks a question and, while concentrating upon it, performs a mechanical operation. This involves the throwing of coins whereby 'heads' stands for Yang and 'tails' for Yin or the more traditional manipulation of yarrow stalks. This gives one a particular hexagram and may well add special points to note and reference to a second hexagram into which the matter changes. One then takes up an I-Ching text; there are many versions. The text consists of 'The Title' (of the hexagram), 'The Decision', 'The Commentary' (by the Duke of Chou, a disciple of Confucius), sometimes unnecessary commentaries by subsequent editors, and 'The Image' it evokes. Accompanying it, there is a comment declaring how 'the superior man' would act. This 'superior man' is one in accordance with Tao Teh. Finally, there is an analysis of each individual line of the hexagram with commentary by the Duke of Chou.

Those who use the I-Ching find it to be extraordinarily wise and helpful in the conduct of life and this was certainly the case, for example, with Aleister Crowley, who consulted it consistently, often daily, and endeavoured to marry himself to the wisdom contained therein. Nor was he the only great Westerner to extol its virtues. The mathematician and philosopher Leibniz instantly perceived that the I-Ching was predicated on binary mathematics, which he thought he alone had discovered, and this greatly impressed him. Carl Jung gave great honour and respect to the I-Ching and, with Richard Wilhelm, was responsible for a laudable and widely known edition.

It was Crowley who managed the difficult and remarkable feat of equating Chinese conceptions with the Qabalistic Tree of Life in a manner which makes absolute sense and sheds new light on both. This equation was published in *The Book of Thoth*. Tao is equated with the Qabalistic Ain (0 or Nothing). Tao manifests as Tao Teh — 1, Kether, The Point. The second Sephirah, Chokmah, masculine, is equated with Yang. The third Sephirah, Binah, feminine, is equated with Yin. United, Yang and Yin, Chokmah and Binah, manifest as all created things. Here is the correspondence with the Tree of Life; note that Daath is used.

1

TAO TEH
KETHER

3
-- --
YIN
BINAH

2
——
YANG
CHOKMAH

11
☰
CH'IEN
HEAVENLY FATHER
DAATH

5
☳
CHÊN
FIRE
GEBURAH

4
☱
TUI
WATER
CHESED

6
☲
LI
SUN
TIPHARETH

8
☴
SUN
AIR
HOD

7
☶
KÊN
EARTH
NETZACH

9
☵
K'AN
MOON
YESOD

10
☷
K'UN
EARTH MOTHER
MALKUTH

It is instructive to compare the primary symbols of the I-Ching with the corresponding Tarot Trumps as outlined in the Astrology chapter of this work. The student should also bear in mind the interesting fact that just as the Tree of Life is based on 32 (10 Sephiroth and 22 Paths), so the I-Ching is based on $2 \times 32 = 64$ (8 x 8 primary trigrams). These equations between the Chinese and Qabalistic systems of thought make one wonder whether they reflect the structure of the mind and to what extent the structure of the mind reflects in turn the structure of the Universe.

One way of investigating this matter is called Scrying.

CHAPTER 9

Scrying

The following advanced practice should under no circumstances be attempted unless the student can perform The Lesser Banishing Ritual of the Pentagram — a simple ceremony — with which the operation *must* begin and end. For a principal purpose of the Pentagram ritual is to prevent the occurrence of the principal danger of this exercise: obsession. Fortunately, it is virtually impossible to succeed in this operation without some previous experience in the training of the mind, but even so, sloppy technique usually results in unhealthy and unbalanced thought and feeling. The Pentagram is given in the Appendices. The operation is as follows:–

1 – Perform the Lesser Banishing Ritual of the Pentagram.
2 – Sit up straight in a hard-backed chair facing East. Breathe slowly, deeply, regularly; and let the mind be calm.
3 – Close your eyes and picture the Tarot card selected.
4 – Imagine that it is on a door.
5 – Imagine yourself going through that door. (This is rather like *Alice Through the Looking-Glass* and is usually the principal difficulty).
6 – You may find yourself in a strange landscape and encountering all manner of beings. Be continuously aware of your experience — it is rather like a dream — and believe nothing. It may even seem as though you are encountering noble and splendid entities who have messages of great import for you; but it is equally possible that you are just exploring the contents of your unconscious and any great 'revelations' are just you chattering to yourself.
7 – Either the experience will come to an end naturally — i.e. you will wake up as from a dream; or you will choose to end it by withdrawing through an imagined door back to your chair.
8 – Perform the Lesser Banishing Ritual of the Pentagram.
9 – Immediately write down your experience.
10 – Check the symbolism in 777 or a similar work. If what you saw

and heard corresponds with the Tarot card you chose, you have had an experience which has increased your comprehension.

11 – If your data is contradictory — if, for example, you used The Hermit but the dominant colour was bright yellow – you have ben engaged in worthless mental drifting.

It is not proposed to waste space and time by discussing whether these experiences are subjective — i.e. we are exploring the Collective Unconscious within us — or objective — i.e. we are exploring another dimension of reality which is usually termed 'the Astral plane'. The question is open and the matter is still debated by the most advanced students, whose opinions differ. This does not matter. By doing certain things, certain things happen.

Of greater interest and more capable of rational explanation is the question of correspondences. Persistent experimentation has demonstrated that in the practice of scrying, we encounter the symbols set forth in theory. In other words, the Tarot really does reflect the contents and structure of our Unconscious; and if there is indeed the Astral Plane, it is an accurate map.

Scrying is sometimes called 'Path Working', since we are exploring the Paths between the various Sephiroth, but the latter term is also used to denote one or more of three practices undertaken by groups. Here they are:–

A ~ Responses

1 – A particular card is chosen and each member of the group has it before him or her. Alternatively, everyone focuses on a projected slide.

2 – After a period of silence during which each member tries to enter the world of the key, it is taken in turn for each one to voice the experience. This can be extremely enjoyable; one could try it as a party game. However, it has two disadvantages. Firstly, weaker members are all too likely to be unduly influenced by the words of others rather than report their own experience, which alone gives merit to the exercise. For instance, it is difficult to imagine someone saying: 'I'm not getting a thing,' though it is vital to say this if it is the truth. Secondly, the exercise can all too easily degenerate into unproductive, egotistical fantasy and woolly, self-indulgent ramblings masquerading as spiritual insight.

B ~ Guidance

1 – A Guide is appointed by the group. This must be a person with some detailed knowledge of Tarot correspondences.

2 – Once again, each member concentrates on the key agreed upon by the group.

3 – The Guide voices the various correspondences, including short tales of mythology.

4 – There is a period of silence during which each member tries to explore the world of the card.

5 – Each person then writes down the experience.

6 – These experiences are then compared.

C ~ Drama

1 – A card is chosen by the group.

2 – A short play or ritual is then created to embody the forces within the card. It can include relevant poetry; also music.

3 – One way is for someone to play the Candidate for Initiation while the others personify the beings in the card and instruct the Candidate.

4 – *The Complete Golden Dawn System of Magic* gives fine examples of this technique in its initiatory rituals.

5 – The precise formulation of this method, however, is best left to the practitioners' ingenium.

The primary disadvantage of group working consists of the difficulty in finding suitable people with whom to work. One should never work with people whom one would dislike in an ordinary social context: the fact that they like Tarot too simply isn't good enough if one is to work with them in delicate operations. Also avoid all groups which charge you a lot of money, or are run by a 'guru-figure' who wants some measure of control over your private life. Your private life is entirely your own affair. Any group which makes the slightest suggestion that it should have influence over it, should be shunned as one would shun a leper. The only groups worth joining are associations of individuals who have come together freely for a common purpose. You will be fortunate indeed to find one of these.

Individual practice and personal study form the spine of spiritual attainment. To further these, I give two more exercises. Firstly, try making your own cards, especially the Major Trumps. Compare these, when done, with your favourite deck and with other decks. On no account be deterred by fears that your draughtsmanship is hopeless or any supposed lack of artistic ability. Here the effort is all. Contrast your own recension with the established work of others, noting the similarities and differences, especially the symbols you have stressed and those you have ignored.

Secondly, take all the knowledge you have of the Tree of Life, especially in view of the Tarot, and go on an imaginative journey from Malkuth to Kether via the cards. You may well have done this on one plane by playing The Royal Game of Human Life as described in Chapter Two. Now do it in your own imagination.

Let us end this Chapter, therefore, with respectful remembrance of Mathers and the Golden Dawn, who demonstrated that the Tarot is a universal and coherent system of hieroglyphs: and with a salute to Aleister Crowley, who developed the work and made the greatest contribution to its evolved understanding in the first half of the twentieth century.

'78.
WHEEL AND — WOA!

The Great Wheel of Samsara.

The Wheel of the Law (Dhamma).

The Wheel of the Taro.

The Wheel of the Heavens.

The Wheel of Life.

All these Wheels be one; yet of all these the Wheel of the TARO alone avails thee consciously.

Meditate long and broad and deep, O man, upon this Wheel, revolving it in thy mind!

Be this thy task, to see how each card springs necessarily from each other card, even in due order from The Fool unto The Ten of Coins. Then, when thou know'st the Wheel of Destiny complete, mayst thou perceive THAT Will which moved it first. (There is no first or last). And lo! thou art past through the Abyss.'

(*The Book of Lies*: Which Is Also Falsely Called Breaks: The Wanderings or Falsifications of The One Thought of Frater Perdurabo Which Thought Is Itself Untrue.)

PART II

CHAPTER 10

Tarot And The Mind

Among other things, the Tarot is an extraordinary guide to the workings of consciousness. More, it can guide us in realising our own deepest potential.

How come? Really, what can we learn here? The reader is cordially invited to take a guided tour of the mind, which mind, it has been suggested, reflects the structure of the Universe. The more we understand ourselves, the more we understand the Universe around us. Any information as to how we can do this is therefore valuable — and it is the present author's contention that this information is supplied by the Tarot.

We start on Earth and rightly. It is no use at all having our heads in the sky if our feet are not on the ground. If you don't get the basics right, you will get nothing right at all. This is all very well and any sane human being would agree — but does the Tarot reflect this basic truth?

It does so very simply and clearly. The Ten of Disks is called Wealth. There is nothing wrong with making money — there is everything wrong with believing that this is the only objective in life. One can see this with brutal accuracy in the evil social effects consequent upon any society accepting money, not as a medium of exchange, but as a measure of personal worth — corruption, crime, prostitution of both body and mind and a total absence of moral values. Too many who achieve wealth find their coffers to be full and their selves to be empty.

The Ten of Swords, Ruin, shows the effects of fighting to no purpose, which is done daily by far too many.

The Ten of Cups, Satiety, shows that if one immerses oneself in materialism without any consciousness of spirit, one will feel jaded at best and (again) empty at worst.

The Ten of Wands displays (among other things) the condition of human beings at the end of the 1980's, that disgusting decade of cowering and abasement, and it is called Oppression. In ten years of despicable grovelling, Man and Woman have been degraded. The card also declares that if we cannot raise our eyes to the stars, we will have our snouts in a trough. At present, the life of homo sapiens in the Third World is largely nasty, brutish and short. In the West it is largely nasty, brutish and long.

It is surely obvious to any thinking person that the 1990's will witness all matters of human survival coming to a crisis. The planet could blow through the stupidity of its leaders — we could all perish in nuclear war. Alternatively, we could rape the Earth on which we live and poison ourselves to death slowly and painfully — an unappealing prospect. Or we could go forward to the stars, which is surely part of our destiny, and assist the acceleration of evolution on what must surely be one of the most beautiful planets in the Milky Way.

This might sound a little too much to the casual reader, perhaps, but certain propositions cannot be denied. The Tarot informs us that the life of the average man on Earth consists of the pursuit of and rule by Wealth, the constant threat of Ruin, the sheer boredom of Satiety and the omnipresence of Oppression.

This is all most unpleasant — but it is what faced the average man and woman during the wretched and miserable 1980's. Is there a way out? Yes, there is. The Tarot declares simply that there is something more to life. It is called The Universe, the Major Trump numbered XXI. It leads from the life of Man on Earth, called Malkuth on the Tree of Life, to the stars.

It is necessary, therefore, to become aware of those aspects of Life which are more than merely 'birth, copulation and death' (to use T.S. Eliot's phrase) on a chunk of rock on which crawl impure lumps of carbon and water, spinning somewhere in the blackness of meaningless space. We can do so by awakening the subconscious. XXI The Universe indicates how this can best be done. The Woman/Goddess at the centre of the card is usually portrayed as surrounded by the four Kerubim, the Lion, the Man, the Eagle and the Bull. These represent the Four Elements by which we can classify life on Earth: and also the Four Powers of the Sphinx by which we can awaken — to Know, to Will, to Dare and to Keep Silent. We are reminded too of the basic truth, fully understood by the ancient Egyptians, that we must accept ourselves as animals before we can realise ourselves as Gods.

The Woman/Goddess in the centre of the card reminds one that the nature of Existence is pure joy. Our paths to this ecstasy consist of expanding our minds outwards to Infinite Space and inwards to explore the Universe of our own Unconscious.

The Four Nines give us further information on Yesod, the ninth Sephirah, which relates to the subconscious especially in its sexual manifestation. The Nine of Wands, Strength, makes the vital point that our sexuality is the basis of our creativity and continued evolution. The Nine of Cups, Happiness, symbolises here the ambition of the average man and woman to enjoy marital bliss. The Nine of Swords, Cruelty, shows the direct result of sexual repression. The Nine of Disks, Gain, shows the initial result of expanded awareness.

However, Yesod is only our first resting place; it is very, very far from being the goal. We will have to go through the experience portrayed by XX The Aeon. In this context — and the reader must bear in mind that this is simply one among a number of ways of regarding the Tarot — it could be said that The Aeon symbolises the destruction of the Universe by fire. This is in fact the result of persistence at any valid magical or mystical discipline: the opening up of new levels of awareness destroys old notions of one's limitations, and burns up stale preconceptions and useless prejudices. One is reborn, as it were, in the eighth Sephirah, Hod, sphere of the Intellect, with a new ideological framework.

This exhilaration is dramatically portrayed by XIX The Sun, which leads from Yesod to Hod.

The expansion of awareness, accompanied as it is by the discarding of those old ideas which were shackles upon one's mental powers, leads to an ecstatic eruption of joyous, subconscious energies. As The Sun shows, contact is made again with the glorious feelings of childhood. One experiences William

Blake's truth that: 'Energy is eternal delight and is of the body.'

In the state of Hod, it is the task of the Aspirant to discipline and control the conscious mind. This is no easy task. As the Eight of Wands, Swiftness, shows us, the mind moves so fast, jumping from one idea to another, that it is very difficult even to observe one's own mental processes calmly. This practice is essential, however; the Yogis call it Pratyahara; for when we gain some comprehension of how the mind works, we become the masters not the victims of its speed.

The Eight of Cups nevertheless demonstrates a special danger of Hod, Indolence. One's initial successes can lead to a rest upon one's laurels and nothing further is accomplished. Again, facility of intellect can lead one to the temptation whereby one thinks it unnecessary to work hard at anything and once again, all progress stops. The Eight of Swords, Interference, displays the tendency of the mind to impede one's Will to Self-Actualisation through its continuous changes: disciplined concentration upon a one-pointed objective is the only answer here. The card also informs us that once we have reached a certain stage, we normally find a hundred reasons, external and internal, for putting off the arduous labours of the next stage until some time after the middle of next week. This problem is answered by the Eight of Disks, Prudence. We must labour patiently and without a squandering of energy if the Tree of Self we are cultivating is to bear edible fruit.

Very well: we have opened up to our sexuality and changed our minds but there is also the matter of our emotions. Once again, the first way is through the subconscious as we go from Malkuth to the seventh Sephirah, Netzach, via XVIII The Moon, but this is where far too many go wrong. Their experiences have been so extraordinary by comparison with the banalities of so-called 'everyday life' that, as Crowley puts it, 'semi-educated stutterers wallow in oceans of gush'. The Tarot demands the employment of one's creative imagination: yet too many drift into a sterile world of unproductive fantasy. There are great schemes and great dreams aplenty but nothing ever comes of them. Some even let their scrying degenerate so abominably that internal mental chatter is mistaken for great revelations by the Gods or Hidden Masters and they become what Francis King aptly termed 'astral junkies'. Crowley's remarks in *MAGICK: In Theory and Practice* summarise the dangers here.

'The Magician may go on for a long time being fooled and flattered by the Astrals that he has himself modified or manufactured. Their natural subservience to himself will please him, poor ape.'

'They will pretend to show him marvellous mysteries, pageants of beauty and wonder unspeakably splendid; he will incline to accept them as true, for the very reason that they are images of himself idealised by imagination.'

'But his real progress will stop dead. These phantasms will prevent him from coming into contact with independent intelligences, from whom alone he can learn anything new.'

'He will become increasingly interested in himself, imagine himself to be attaining one initiation after another. His Ego will expand unchecked, till he seem to himself to have heaven at his feet. Yet all this will be nothing but his fool's face of Narcissus smirking up from the pool that will drown him.'

Fortunately, in the Crowley-Harris portrayal of The Moon, there is shown the way through: it is identification with the sun at midnight, that is to say, the Will — and this must be done even and especially during those moods of anxiety and depression which afflict the aspirant.

This message is reinforced by IV The Emperor, which leads from Yesod to Netzach. We are trying to become fully aware of our feelings; the greatest of these feelings is Love; yet as it is written in *The Book of the Law*, 'Love is the law, love under will'. The nature of the Universe is Love, or the urge for union between opposites, but for each one, that Love must be in accordance with the True Will of the individual. The only true discipline is self-discipline and, as The Emperor shows, that is precisely what is required here. Coming from Yesod, the aspirant must ride upon his/her sexuality as a strong human being masters a stallion.

Yet one's difficulties are far from over. The struggles of the Will to break through the snares of fantasy, distraction and notions of vague sentimentality have their effect in Hod (the Intellect) and this effect is shown by XVI The Tower, which leads from Hod to Netzach. At this stage, the consciousness of heightened and deepened awareness often blasts the aspirant's most preciously held convictions. The ego is not annihilated at this stage but it frequently feels as though it has been and there ensues a state of confusion.

The ancient qabalists did not name Netzach 'external splendour and internal corruption' for nothing, as the Four Sevens demonstrate. One sought to identify with one's feelings only to discover one has precious little idea of what those feelings genuinely are. The Seven of Wands, Valour, is that to which one must cling during this excruciatingly difficult stage, part of which is the putrefaction summarised by the Seven of Cups, Debauch. One is all too likely to collapse for a time. The Seven of Swords shows the consequent conviction of Futility and is succeeded by the Seven of Disks, Failure. The Great Work seems worthless — and so does everything else. Why did one bother in the first place? All that work, all that excitement — and now one feels only a numb bitterness.

The only way out of this appalling state is to persist in aspiration towards a conception greater than the personal ego — it is immaterial which word or phrase is used as nomenclature for this conception.

To this end, we must return to Yesod on the Middle Pillar of the Tree of Life and employ methods given by XIV Art, which one could summarise by the aphorism of the Alchemists: 'Solve et Coagula'. We must dissolve the self — the personal ego — and recombine its elements.

There is a formula known as IAO — Isis-Apophis-Osiris — which expresses the process involved here. In beginning any set of practices for self-improvement, there is a first or Isis stage. The work seems pleasant, easy, exciting and delightful. This is soon enough succeeded by the Apophis stage: one reacts to the work with infinite weariness and detestation. Nothing goes well at all. However, further persistence is rewarded by the Osiris stage: a glorious resurrection of both aspiration and results.

The work of XIV Art begins with the putrefaction that has followed upon initial joys. It is our task to analyse the nature of that putrefaction. Then we must do something about it. Normally it is found that any problem consists of three elements — two opposites and their resolution. One finds this notion also in Marxist dialectic as derived from Hegel — thesis, antithesis and synthesis. Here and specifically, we have a conflict between Intellect and Emotion to be resolved by deeper awareness of the Unconscious. We must sharpen our intellect, purify our feelings and resolve all conflicts at a deeper level of awareness while keeping the body healthy and directing our sexuality towards the highest we can imagine. With all our faculties harmonised, we can set out from Yesod towards the sixth Sephirah, Tiphareth, which is the centre of the Tree of Life and the seat of Higher Consciousness. As Crowley commented, we must fire ourselves at this state like a straight arrow.

Our intellect, though sharp as a razor, must not be allowed to get in the way. It is a splendid servant but a bad master. This is one of many meanings of the Path which leads from Hod to Tiphareth, XV The Devil. This experience involves the realisation, nobly expressed once again by William Blake, that 'everything that lives is holy'. We must fully accept our own sexuality and that of the Universe for, as the artist and magician Austin Osman Spare wrote: 'All things fornicate all the time.' We must accept that many truths about the Universe are shocking to the average ego. And we must face what has been called The Dweller on the Threshold.

Coming to know God — or the attainment of Superconsciousness or whatever sectarian terms is preferred — is for most a terrifying experience which evokes every possible dread and element of paranoia from the psyche. It takes a while to comprehend that all one's intellectual conceptions, arrived at after agonies, are still inadequate. Many find that their lives go haywire at this point, that the Universe proceeds to behave in a manner contrary to all the known rules of Physics and Psychology as accepted by the most learned men and women of humanity. You will probably have to face your own deepest fears — and not in your head, which will in any case be sufficiently bombarded by perplexing data, but in the events of daily living.

But let us suppose that you have the courage to persist. You accept your sexuality, you expand your mind, you allow yourself to feel your emotions reverberating truly in your heart and you harmonise all these in the true work of Netzach. Splendid! Surely you are ready for the next stage? Not on your life.

For the next stage is Death.

XIII Death leads from Netzach to Tiphareth, the sixth Sephirah of Beauty, Harmony, Self-Actualisation and, as some call it, the Knowledge and Conversation of the Holy Guardian Angel. In order to attain it, the harmonised Personality must die so as to experience a far deeper Individuality. All that you have gained must be annihilated, sacrificed, given — to something greater, to the Self far greater than anything you ever called your self.

This is the greatest experience open to the majority of men and women on this planet. It is, for the time being, the goal of evolution. The harmonised faculties of body, sexuality, intellect and emotion are sacrificed to and then adorned by the nobility of aware Spirit. Once that has been done, one knows one's True Will in the World. Do what thou wilt shall be the whole of the Law.

This foremost axiom of *The Book of the Law* does *not* mean anything as trite and silly as 'Do what you want'. It means that you are on this planet for a purpose. This purpose might be anything. It could mean the painting of pictures or the writing of books but it could also mean a career in Chartered Accountancy. It could mean professional boxing or business or carpentry or television comedy. It could equally well mean that your Will is ultimately to be a fine parent of a remarkable child. You know your True Will by the extraordinary joy you experience in doing it — and you will discover that mere wants interfere with the Will. As Crowley rightly has it in *MAGICK WITHOUT TEARS*:

'If there is any truth at all in anything, or even any meaning in life, in Nature herself; then there is one thing, one thing only paramount; to find out who one is, what is one's necessary Way.'

'The alternative to the Great Work is the hotchpotch of dispersion, of fatuity, or disconnected nonsense'.

The rewards of the Great Work are succinctly stated in the four Sixes. The Six of Wands displays Victory of the Will over all that has impeded it. The Six of Cups is called Pleasure and rightly so. The Six of Swords, Science, shows the human mind raised to its highest power of intellectual penetration. The Six of Disks is simply Success.

There is a word for this attainment: Adeptship. An Adept is one who has brought all his or her faculties to an heightened realisation of purpose in life through the experience of super-consciousness. Each system has its own ways of classifying levels of development but it may fairly be stated that they can all be reduced to four: Student; Initiate; Adept; and Master. A Student studies ways of evolving. An Initiate is experienced in the actual practice of these ways. An Adept has discovered the True Will within and can put this into action despite the many restrictions of our society. For the present it is best not to speak of a Master — there are very few of them.

The task of the new Adept — or, if the reader prefers, an enlightened and evolved person — is first to perfect that Adeptship. This is no easy task. Adeptship is a great attainment. One could hardly be blamed for remaining in that state. Yet there is the call to come farther up and further in. Naturally the Tarot shows how.

XII The Hanged Man, which leads from Hod 8 (Intellect) to Geburah 5 (Force), has baffled a number of commentators. It could be argued that for once, Crowley allowed his personal antipathy towards the Christian faith to interfere with judicious observation. For the Key expresses the central mystery of Western religion over the past two thousand years: that there was a God-Man who died and rose again, known variously around the Mediterranean basin as Osiris, Adonis, Attis, Dionysus and Jesus Christ, under whose name the various competing cults were subsumed. This cult is essentially solar and based upon the superstition of two thousand years ago and before, that the Sun died every night and required worship, prayers and magic in order for it to be reborn. These days we know that to be nonsense — the Sun is there all the time whatever we do. Obviously any religion should reflect this reality.

The Hanged Man has clearly outlived his usefulness on that level. Significantly, he appears in the twentieth century's greatest poetic expression of pessimism, *The Waste Land* by T.S. Eliot.

'I do not find The Hanged Man
Fear death by water.'

And as the attentive reader may recall, The Hanged Man corresponds to the Hebrew letter Mem, which means water, and of which correspondence Eliot was unaware when writing the poem — a curious example of synchronicity.

But is The Hanged Man of any possible use to us today? The present writer would respectfully disagree with Crowley and argue that it is. After all, New Aeon or not, it expresses the relation between 8 and 5 and the corresponding psychological reality. One way of regarding the matter is in terms of ordeals. If you try to liberate yourself, the pain can be excruciating.

'Now just as the Aspirant, on the Threshold of Initiation, finds himself assailed by the "complexes" which have corrupted him, their externalisation excruciating him, and his agonised reluctance to their elimination plunging him into such ordeals that he seems (both to himself and to others) to have turned from a noble and upright man into an unutterable scoundrel; so does the *First Matter* blacken and putrefy as the Alchemist breaks up its coagulations of impurity.'

(Crowley: *MAGICK: In Theory and Practice*.)

The nature of 5 Geburah is Fire and in order to advance one's Adeptship, all remaining impurities must be sacrificed as burned offerings and consumed by something greater than oneself. Obviously this process is painful.

VIII Adjustment also leads to 5 Geburah but from 6 Tiphareth in which one should be centred. In order to progress, there must be equilibrium of the Self. There has to be a balanced poise. There are a number of ways of achieving this. One is a dispassionate mating of every idea and tendency within oneself with its opposite. Another is a refusal to undertake any action unless it is necessary to the fulfilment of the Will or the immediate task in hand, which should amount to the same thing. Any Adept worth a pinch of salt should be capable of devising further methods.

The experience of the naked Force of Geburah is not easy to handle. The Five of Wands, Strife, declares the conflicts that will arise, both within the self and within the environment. The Five of Cups shows all false illusions dropping away in Disappointment. The Five of Swords makes it clear that the pursuit of individual power, so tempting to many at this point, can only lead to its title, Defeat. There is bound to be a period of self-questioning and, as the Five of Disks has it, Worry.

The Adept will once again have to return to original aspiration founded in truth of feeling. The Universe is indeed like the wheel portrayed in X Fortune, which leads from 7 Netzach to the next destination, 4 Chesed (Form), but it must be realised that the place to be is not whirling around on the wheel but at the very centre, the ultimate point of which does not move at all. One could learn so much and feel so good if only one could sit still and be quiet.

This message is reinforced by IX The Hermit which takes one from 6 Tiphareth to 4 Chesed. It is the True Will, the Silent Self within us, which moves us to go on: it is also the Light before us which calls us to come on. It is that which was pure in the beginning and will be pure, though infinitely more experienced and therefore greater at the end.

To this end we must be aware of IT and mate IT within us to All that exists without us, rejoicing in the ecstasy and comedy of Existence, as shown in XI Lust. Only through appreciation of the divine spasms of every moment of life can the cells within us attain full potential.

A glorious state awaits those who succeed. The Four of Wands signifies Completion: the Adept has brought Adeptship to its highest perfection. In consequence, there is the Four of Cups, Luxury, to be enjoyed. This may occur in the usual, vulgar sense of the word: though some perfected Adepts rejoice in the unashamed luxury of a hunk of freshly baked bread and a glass of good, pure water, finding here greater delights than the gourmet dining of the fastidious epicure. This is hardly surprising, since the Four of Swords, Truce, displays the psyche at peace with itself. The Four of Disks declares the reward: Power. This may come through in many ways: individual charisma;

a work of art or science; remarkable business aptitude; sporting proficiency or media presence — one might even be famous for being famous on account of nothing in particular. In any event, a lasting mark is made upon the environment.   Now comes the greatest crisis of all. Having attained to the supreme level of Adeptship possible to any human being, you have to give up all that you have and all that you are to the Universe Itself. You even have to give up your preciously won super-consciousness.

'You have to leave the House of Love, as they call the Fourth House. You are quite, quite naked; you must take off your husband-clothes, and your baby-clothes, and all your pleasure-clothes, and your skin, and your flesh, and your bones, every one of them must come right off. And then you must take off your feeling clothes; and then your idea clothes; and then what we call your tendency clothes which you have always worn and which make you what you are. After that you take off your consciousness clothes, which you have always thought were your very own self, and you leap out into the cold abyss, and you can't think how lonely it is. There isn't any light, or any path, or anything to catch hold of to help you, and there is no Fairy Prince any more: you can't even hear his voice calling you to come on. There's nothing to tell you which way to go, and you feel the most horrible sensation of falling away from everything that ever was. You've got no nothing at all; you don't know how awful it all is. You would turn back if you could only stop falling; but luckily you can't. So you fall faster and faster; and I can't tell you any more.'

(Crowley: *The Wake World* from *Konx Om Pax*.)

Once again the Tarot is the supreme guide to this, the greatest crisis of all initiations. There is no path from 4 to 3. You just have to take a leap in the dark, as the Existentialists advocate. And if one grain of ego remains, the result will be not a Master but a monster. All that can bring one through is Love, given freely and without condition, to and for All.

It is hardly surprising, therefore, that the path which leads to 3 (Understanding) from the Beauty and Harmony of 6 is portrayed by VI The Lovers. The experience is not termed a

Mystic Marriage for nothing. You have to mate the deepest and finest and grandest within you with All without you.

Here one should remind the reader of Crowley's $0 = 2$ equation, which expresses the nature of the Universe. It is the shortest and simplest way of expressing: $0 = (+1) + (-1)$. If we look at the manifested Universe, we find that each and every phenomenon has its opposite. In other words, as the Yin-Yang symbol informs us, the Universe manifests as pairs of opposites: male and female, positive and negative. If we put these pairs of opposites together, they cancel out to Nothing. Hence $0 = 2$. And hence The Lovers, in which the opposites are mated and annihilation ensues.

Our second guide through the Abyss between Actual and Ideal is VII The Chariot. The path runs from 5 to 3. The charioteer is armed with all weapons but he bears the Holy Graal into which one must give every last drop of one's own blood, keeping back nothing. This truth is stated time and time again in the magnificent tales of the quest for the Holy Graal: Malory's *Morte d'Arthur* (*Not* Tennyson's) is its supreme expression in English. King Arthur's knights are the bravest, toughest, most intelligent and most chivalrous beings on the earth but they must give up their all for the Holy Graal.

There has been a foreshadowing of this in Atu XI Lust, in which Our Lady BABALON who rides upon The Beast bears the Holy Graal filled with the blood of the saints whom She has slaughtered. One is reminded of an American book, written many years ago for women but equally applicable to men; it is called *The Power of Sexual Surrender*.

In Sir Thomas Malory's recension of the Graal Quest, only four knights reach the stage of The Chariot. Sir Lancelot receives a vision of the Graal but cannot go further, for his adultery with Guinevere is no trivial sexual adventure; it is a betrayal of his Oath of Loyalty sworn to his King. In Magick, you cannot break an Oath. Sir Galahad, the Pure Fool, comes to the Graal and dies. One does. And if the death is physical, one would welcome it. Others like Sir Galahad are simply silent.

Sir Perceval comes to the Graal after which he is a hermit for a year. As Voltaire recommends, he cultivates his own garden.

Then he dies willingly and gladly. The cases of Sir Galahad and Sir Perceval have their parallels in Theravada (Hinayana) Buddhism, whereby the ideal is to become an Arhat, one who has attained unto that Nothingness which is termed Nirvana.

However, in Mayahana Buddhism the ideal is to become a Bodhisattva, one who will not accept the reward of Nirvana until all sentient beings have equally attained. In Malory's account, this is symbolised by Sir Bors, who must be a hermit for a year, then return to the court of King Arthur to recount his experiences. This too is the case with the majority of Adepts who reach the exalted state of Master. Yet it is not exalted, for there is Nothing to exalt. There is just a little pile of dust and ashes; but a star is ignited below the Abyss and within the human being and it lives and moves and has its being, to all appearances being no different from anyone else.

A cautionary word is in order here. In the Western Tradition, there is something called the Oath of the Abyss. Its most important section consists of swearing to regard each and every event as a dealing between the Universe and the Self. This of course applies to the most trivial matters, including an advertisement seen on television or a change in traffic lights. It would apply also to the event of being given a cup of unsatisfactory tea. It should be obvious to any attentive reader that it is hard to distinguish this state from that of paranoid psychosis, or one induced by a powerful dose of LSD or that of a small child. The last analogy is the closest. It is similar — very similar — to, though not precisely identical with the state of being under consideration. One of the finer sayings attributed to Jesus Christ is: 'Except ye be as little children, ye shall in no wise enter the kingdom of heaven'. In the Western Tradition, it is not for nothing that this state is termed: the Babe of the Abyss.

For 1900 years, the received wisdom was that one did not dare to swear the Oath of the Abyss until one became a perfected Adept in 4. This is sound teaching and still applies — but the twentieth century has witnessed the most extraordinary changes. For a start, there has been more technological change than in the preceding 1900 years put together. Also, times are critical to the survival of this planet. Therefore there has been an acceleration of evolution and certain time honoured rules have been relaxed. In consequence, as Crowley stated, anyone genuinely on the Path can at any stage swear this Oath of the Abyss.

Anyone who does so runs the most appalling risks. Indeed, the present writer would argue strongly for the maintenance of traditional wisdom on the grounds that he does not like the casualty lists. For if you do it at the wrong time and for the wrong reasons, you will be back to the Ten of Swords (Ruin) and all your good work will be reduced to rubble. The usual penalties for the abuse of Magick and Mysticism are total loss of common sense, complete absence of humour, rage at the slightest criticism and egotistical megalomania. This is all too likely at the earliest stages but here the disease must be witnessed to be believed.

We can find an excellent case study of this phenomenon in Frater Achad, Charles Stansfield Jones, a leading disciple of Aleister Crowley. He got down to work with the earnest, practical self-discipline which distinguishes the best Americans. His early diaries, published in *The Equinox III 1* (aka *The Blue Equinox*) are fine examples of what a magical diary should be and one's study is greatly augmented by the comments of Major Fuller — his supervisor and later a Major-General and creator of *Blitzkrieg* — and more so, Aleister Crowley. In America 1915, Crowley performed an operation with one 'Sister Hilarion' (aka Jeanne Foster) — to beget 'a magical Son'. In complete ignorance of this Operation and precisely nine months later, Frater Achad (Unity) swore the Oath of the Abyss and became a Babe therein.

At first, it seemed that all was well. Achad/Jones discovered the mathematical key to *The Book of the Law* — that extraordinary document dictated to Crowley in Cairo April 1904 by a praeter-human Intelligence — which key is 31. This technical matter is beyond the scope of this treatise. It suffices to state that the matter was predicted in *The Book of the Law* itself.

Yet after that, Achad went wrong. After writing some very fine work on Qabalah and his wondrous *Hymns to the Star Goddess*, it is fair to state that he made a complete prat of himself. He inverted all the paths on the Qabalistic Tree of Life — with no discernible benefit to anyone, including and especially himself. He went around 'dispelling the veils of illusion.' In theory, this is sound. In his practice, it was not, for he wandered about the streets, naked beneath a raincoat, doing what any sane person would call 'flashing', to the great shame of all connected with him. For a time he joined the Roman Catholic Church, hoping forlornly to convert an organisation predicated upon the pitiful and evil notions of guilt and sin to a way which regards these as disgusting perversions: needless to say, he made no headway there. The classic tale of the Jones/Achad folly and fatuity has been related in one of the many excellent books of Francis King. Jones was trying to mend his car in the street. He tried for many hours over two weeks without any success. Finally a neighbour who knew of Jones' veneration for Crowley sarcastically suggested that a reading of The Master's poetry to the car might mend matters.

'I've tried that,' said Jones, 'and she just drips oil.'

In a final burst of inanity, Jones/Achad announced in the late Forties that the Age of Horus the Child, Horus the God of War, Horus the God Who states that we must realise ourselves as animals before we can become as Gods and Goddesses, the Age prophesied by Crowley to follow the Age of the Mother and the Age of the Father — Isis and Osiris — had been aborted before it had even properly got started; and was abolished in favour of the Aeon of Maat — portrayed in Atu VIII Adjustment — the Aeon of Truth and Justice. This is indeed prophesied in *The Book of the Law* to follow the Aeon of Horus and of course one looks forward to its appearance within some hundreds of years — but any newspaper can inform one that it is not here now and anyone who thinks it is can neither see with eyes nor hear with ears. If we want that to come about, we will have to fight and fuck for it. That is what the Aeon of Horus is about. We must liberate ourselves from external and internal tyranny by fighting, then come closer to one another by fucking. With Love we can come through this critical transition and make a better world.

The Book of the Law abolishes itself at the right time, unlike any other prophetic writing. It gives us the Signs for which we must look in its Third Chapter, Verse 34.

'But your holy place shall be untouched throughout the centuries: though with fire and sword it be burnt down & shattered, yet an invisible house there standeth, and shall stand until the fall of the Great Equinox; when Hrumachis shall arise and the double-wanded one assume my throne and place. Another prophet shall arise, and bring fresh fever from the skies; another woman shall awake the lust & worship of the Snake; another soul of God and beast shall mingle in the globed priest; another sacrifice shall stain the tomb; another king shall reign; and blessing no longer be poured To the Hawk-headed mystical Lord!'

Where did Achad/Jones go wrong? Most would argue that he took the Oath of the Abyss at 10 (Malkuth) — an admitted fact — and the quantum jump into 3 (Understanding) was too much for him; he had not learned enough to be worth annihilation. Or else, he did it for the worst possible reason — he wanted to be a Master. If you want to be a Master, you haven't a hope in hell. Your desire is the measure of your egotism.

The present writer has unfortunately witnessed far too many promising candidates adding their names to the casualty list out of a silly desire for Mastership. The result is a bunch of maladjusted, malcontented, misaligned nincompoops knowing little but thinking they know all and imposing on the gullible with psychological tricks while they wander away in the waste.

Too many forget that within each Sephirah of the Tree of Life there is another Tree. Many do indeed cross an Abyss and often: but they fail to realise that they have only crossed it in 10 or 9 or 8 or 7 or higher — and you must cross it again and again and again. Do it for its own sake. If any part of your motive to be a Master — forget it. You'll never get there. You haven't got it. At this stage, even the noblest ambition is an egotistical vice.

The truths which the Tarot states about 3 — Binah, Understanding, as we must not forget, — apply to the true crossing of the Abyss and therefore also to every crossing within the lower Sephiroth which reflect It. The Three of Wands is called Virtue.

This is a word which has been grossly debased. It is a word exalted by a very popular but very feeble movement called The New Age. One sighs in despair over its fatuity.

This movement is essentially well-intentioned. However, in the critical times in which we live, good intentions alone are definitely not enough; actions must match words and there are few things more contemptible than fine words followed by shabby actions. The present writer is aware that he may have many New Age readers. He regards them as being honestly misguided at best. There is certainly no disgrace in being honestly misguided: it can happen to the best of us. However there is no excuse for not trying to do things better than before.

'Virtue' is a very New Age word. Where does it come from? It comes from the Latin *Vir* — a Man. The Roman *Virtus* therefore expresses healthy, natural male qualities. In these current, degenerate times — which the Hindus rightly call the *Kali Yuga*, the Dark Age — we find a feeble flop in the present comprehension of 'virtue'. Would you rather meet a virtuous man or a virile man? The answer is obvious to all who have not been bemused, abused and confused by ludicrous notions of what it means to be 'spiritual', another New Age buzz word.

The word 'spiritual', which used to mean something important, has like 'virtue' degenerated into meaning something feeble, like a cup of scummy, lukewarm milk. Would you rather meet someone who is spiritual or someone who is spirited? Again, the question is as easy as the answer is obvious.

New Age readers are strongly urged to consider the following propositions, prompted by Virtue — the 3 of Wands in Binah (Understanding) — and certainly not inspired by the sordid motives which enable those with a little but not much occult knowledge or understanding to make money from pandering to the prejudices of said readers. The present writer hopes and trusts that the present reader is not a gullible dupe.

a – New Age is merely softened down and tarted up Christianity; an outmoded religion once adhered to by primitive mammalian primates based upon ludicrous notions of sin and guilt. Under Christianity, perfectly natural desires were called 'sinful'. Under New Age, you still have to be guilty as sin for the same, for the words and phrases are 'unspiritual' — whatever that may mean — or 'not virtuous'. Whatever words are used, people still end up feeling guilty over perfectly natural and honourable feelings like love, hate, lust, anger *et al.*

b – New Age is intellectually sloppy. If you are New Age, you can believe anything you like — as long as it doesn't work.

c – New Age is horribly middle class. In common with any sensible individual, the present writer does not care if you are upper class, middle class or working class: it's just that if you're middle class, you should do something about it. In England, at any rate, the upper classes and the working classes share the same code of honour: observers are confused too often because the same code is expressed in different forms of the English language. Although there are — thank heavens! — exceptions, the average middle class individual has no code of honour. Anyone with no code of honour is a slave. It doesn't matter if your chains are of gold or of plastic — you are still a slave. This is why one can all too often see crass examples such as those who bleat about changing the world, then freak out like a shell-shocked invalid on account of a cigarette being smoked with joy in a Glastonbury tea-room. This is why one can hear whingeing nonsense whenever there is a serious meditation practice from some New Age twits who whine to be excused on the quicksands of: 'Oh — but we're professional meditators.' How is a 'professional' meditator to be distinguished from one who meditates? — apart from the obvious fact that they're probably conning the gullible for money? No. This won't do at all and it's high time someone said so.

d – New Age is dishonest. The beliefs its adherents hold contradict one another. If you are New Age, you can be a Hindu and a Buddhist. Hindus believe that there is a soul (*atman*). Buddhists believe that there isn't (*anatta*). You can't believe both at the same time. Yes, of course, it is said that above the Abyss, all contradictions resolve themselves. This is true — as the Tarot shows us — but the present writer doubts if there are currently more than 93 individuals on the globe capable of mating the contradictions in self-annihilation. Below the Abyss, Reason is King. Facts must be accurate and Logic must be coherent. Unless you get that right, you will get nothing right at all — and New Age doesn't.

e – New Age consists of sentimental slop, catering to half-witted, panic-stricken, middle-class prejudice. The Universe is not like that. Let us remember, therefore, that the Master has spirit and *vir* — and *vir* applies exactly to an acknowledged female Master like Madame Blavatsky — and pass on to the Three of Cups, Abundance. Once you have transcended all that you called your Self, you will be given all that you need. Needs vary. And you yourself must give to those needs, for the more you give, the more it will be renewed. The principal job of the Master who has attained to Understanding is quietly to tend a small garden of disciples who will one day sit alongside him as piles of dust casting forth a star unto Mankind. In the giving is the Abundance, for this Well can never be exhausted.

Appropriately enough, the Three of Swords is called Sorrow, another Name for 3 Binah. In this state of Understanding, one perceives the Pain of Existence. It all seems to be such a waste. There is all this agony — and for what? Hindu theologians have yet to answer the question as to why a Self originally perfect (*atman*) in Nothingness from which all is created (*Brahman*) should enter into manifested Existence (*Maya* = Illusion) solely in order to return intact and perfect to Brahman. Buddhist theologians have yet to explain the point of it all.

Buddhism is the most logically coherent of all the organised religions. Its founder, Gautama — for 'buddha' means simply 'Enlightened One' — the man who was born a Prince and died a beggar for the sake of human evolution, declared Four Noble Truths:–

1 – Existence is Suffering.
2 – The cause of Suffering is Craving.
3 – The cessation of suffering is the cessation of craving.
4 – The Way to this cessation is the following of the Noble Eightfold Path.

This, as any practising Buddhist can inform one, consists of eight principles of conduct and mental training. Buddhism in the form known as Hinayana or Theravada is Southern Buddhism and closest to the original teachings of Gautama. The system is appropriately simple. The idea is to stop existing. Those who imagine that Nirvana implies some kind of self-conscious bliss are merely engaging in a cowardly wish-fulfilment fantasy. If the Wheel of Existence (Samsara) which consists of seemingly endless incarnations, is Suffering, then Nirvana (Non-Existence) shows us the way out. We stop existing.

And Suffering ends.

'Birth is Misery.

Life is Misery.

Death is Misery

But Resurrection is the greatest Misery of all.'

Thus runs the great, time-honoured wisdom of Buddhism. Noble indeed. Yet they still haven't told us the point of it all. We come into suffering in order to stop suffering — well, that makes loadsa sense, doesn't it?

Small wonder that during his Buddhist phase 1901–4, Aleister Crowley sent his friends New Year postcards saying simply: 'Wishing you a speedy termination of Existence.'

In the Three of Swords of the Tarot, one reaches the position advanced by Hume in *A Treatise of Human Nature* and *An Enquiry Concerning Human Understanding*. There is no God and there is no Self and there is no Cause and there is no reason to believe in anything whatsoever. Our minds are formed merely through what Hume calls 'custom and habit'. One could also call it 'genetics and conditioning'.

The clarity of this eighteenth century Scottish philosopher is utterly remarkable — so is the fact that he states Buddhist philosophy and psychology with such precise exactitude. Everything depends on the tendencies of the mind, which tendencies are themselves wholly unpredictable. We might expect an apple to taste like an apple because it has done so one million times before. Yet the next time we may be surprised to find that it tastes like a potato. Moreover, our minds might have changed so much that we expect it to taste like a potato anyway — one never knows. According to Hume — and nobody, but *nobody*, has been able to refute his reasoning, from Kant to Bertrand Russell and after — our conscious beliefs have no basis in fact and anything might happen at any second.

What is the Self? Hume asks. Simply a succession of thoughts and feelings which change constantly and which imply no central unifying idea of 'identity'.

What is 'cause'? Hume asks. Merely an observation of one event usually followed by another event which leads us to assume that there is some mysterious 'causal' connection between them. This sounds as unbelievable as Magick.

The Three of Swords (Sorrow) also covers Hume's final position. Having demonstrated that there is no reason at all to believe in anything whatsoever, he asks honestly whether he himself believes his own writings. Obviously he does at the time of writing, but he confesses that subsequently he will see friends, drink wine and play a game or two of backgammon, which actions will make him as much a creature of custom and habit (i.e. genetics and conditioning) as anyone else. What, then, is the point of Philosophy? Hume answers: just a pleasant way of passing the time.

There is also the Trance of Sorrow. Its nature and its significance to Western Man have been brilliantly explored, for instance, by Colin Wilson in *The Outsider*. The outsider is one who 'sees too deep and too much', becoming in consequence, alienated from the herd and its material concerns; for he is appalled by the futility of all human endeavour. Buddhists call this the Trance of Sorrow. Others might term it 'an existential crisis'. All who have experienced it agree on three points: the feeling is one of bitter agony; eventually one becomes conscious of a ravenous hunger and infinite yearning — suspected in themselves to be futile — for some secret glory which will restore essential meaning to life; and it changes one's fundamental point of view for a lifetime. It is this experience which starts so many upon the Quest. And at this extraordinarily exalted stage of 3 (Binah) we find at this end what was at the beginning, only after a deeper and infinitely more powerful manner.

Finally, if we look objectively at this beautiful planet of ours, we will be tempted to respond to the pain upon it and the sheer stupidity which governs it by crying our eyes out from our heart.

It should be with relief, then, that we dry our eyes, heave a sigh with a great, deep breath — and turn to what we can do about it. This is shown with the utmost clarity by the Three of Disks — Works. Nothing can happen unless there is action. If we wish to improve something, words alone won't do it. Good intentions alone certainly won't achieve anything at all. Work is what counts.

This is a pity — or at least it appears so initially — because work can come over as being such a bore. Sometimes one would rather do anything other than work. One can be like the man who said: 'I love work. I can sit and look at it for hours.' There is also much to be said for what that fine and unjustly neglected artist Arthur Machen insisted upon in praise of idleness, 'concerning which so much cant and false doctrine have been preached.' Even so, only work can make the Ideal Actual.

Today many people like to think that they are enlightened. They might be right. After all, we live in strange times and sometimes miracles do happen. The trouble is that so many of these people who call themselves enlightened don't do anything about it. Little is conveyed to anyone else other than a false sense of superiority. The fact is that it doesn't matter how enlightened you are or how enlightened you may fancy yourself to be: unless you work to earth that enlightenment, the game is not worth the candle.

Aleister Crowley described himself in his *Bibliographical Note* to *The Book of Thoth* as 'the laziest man in three continents!' yet also wrote — and meant it and showed it:

'To advance — that means Work. Patient, exhausting, thankless, often bewildering Work. Dear sister, if you would but Work! Work blindly, foolishly, misguidedly, it doesn't matter in the end: Work in itself has absolute virtue.'

(Magick Without Tears)

Whether we are genuinely at the state of Mastership or whether we are reflecting it through progress on a lower level, the Tree of Life and its Paths as expressed by the Tarot continues to be our guide, philosopher and friend. This is especially true of XVII The Star, the Path which leads from 6, where we centre the Self, to 2 Chokmah (Wisdom) where we have transcended the

Self and are way beyond it. The Star portrays NUIT, Goddess of Infinite Space and the Infinite Stars thereof. In *The Book of the Law* she cries 'To me! To me!' and 'To love me is better than all things,' and 'seek me only! Then the joys of my love will redeem ye from all pain. This is so: I swear it by the vault of my body; by my sacred heart and tongue; by all I can give, by all I desire of ye all.' Finally — at this point-event, for one can only exhort the reader to turn to the original — 'Sing the rapturous love-song unto me! Burn to me perfumes! Wear to me jewels! Drink to me, for I love you! I love you!'

We are always being told that we should go around giving out more love than we do. This is true enough — though in the present writer's experience, the majority of people do a decent job of it under very difficult circumstances. A far greater difficulty is the *acceptance* of love from another. Emotional life is harsh for most. Tough people — who are the best people and usually the most sensitive — somehow still manage to give love yet all too often cannot accept it. It is hard to believe that one could be loved utterly and totally simply for being what one is. Yet this is just what the Goddess does.

Too much nonsense has been written about the Goddess by New Age theologians writing on something called 'Wicca' — it used to be called Witchcraft. They seem to want to give the God castration and the Goddess a clitorectomy. By their accounts, the Goddess of the Stars, sky, moon and earth is a terribly nice, well-intentioned and properly brought up young lady in a floppy, flower-patterned Laura Ashley dress and she smiles a lot, drinks herb tea, says we should all be a bit nicer to one another and implies that too much sex is, well, you know, a bit messy. They make Her sound like the best sort of trendy, schoolteaching nun — though let us not forget that Nun, the Hebrew letter which means Fish, corresponds with the Tarot Trump XIII Death. This notion of the Goddess is a rather silly fib. Whenever it is advanced, the present writer is reminded of the conceited young man who wanted to embarrass the Duke of Wellington socially and who therefore greeted him at some function with the words: 'Good afternoon, sir. Mr. Smith, I believe.' 'If you believe that,' the Iron Duke replied, 'you will believe anything.'

The Goddess can be lethal, lustful and bloodthirsty. The Hindus see this clearly enough in their worship of Kali. Yet the Goddess can also be the gentlest, greatest and most loving force in the Universe. All we have to do is accept Her Love.

If we can do that, if we can only comprehend that in the stars without us, there is something infinitely greater and infinitely more loving to which we aspire, then we can move from the quiet passivity of Understanding in 3 to the active Wisdom of 2.

In order to do that successfully, we will need V The Hierophant, which Path leads from 4 to 2. On one level — and it should be obvious by now that one of the principal joys of the Tarot is that it is multi-levelled — the Hierophant stands for the Teacher or Guru who gets you to learn how to join him as an equal. The trouble is that there are very few of these people about who are genuine. The few who are, will probably show complete disinterest in keen students anyway. They are sick and tired of casting pearls before swine, of being energised by fine words then disillusioned by shabby actions. Probably these days they will tell you to go away and do some work and ask them if you have any questions. Asking people to do some work is the best way of getting rid of useless wastrels.

These extraordinary people, who are very hard to find, are nothing like the vast majority who pose as 'teachers' or 'masters'. You can spot these latter and disgraceful sorts fairly simply: they always want to have power over you. As the seventh Earl of Tankerville (unjustly?) accused Aleister Crowley: 'I'm sick of you always teaching, teaching, teaching, as if you were God Almighty and I were some poor, bloody shit in the street.'

These charlatans and posturing clowns, whom one is all too likely to meet on the occult scene, should be shunned more than one would shun HIV carriers. You might be lucky enough to meet a genuine Teacher, though you probably won't unless it's essential and you're ready for it. There's nothing you can do about it anyway. Many advance through discarnate teachers: here I refer not to mysterious entities whose very existence is a matter for debate, but to the authors of good writings. As Lord Macauley rightly stated: 'A good book is the precious life-blood of a master spirit.'

95

Finally, as the late Dr. Israel Regardie insisted to me time and time again, the best teacher of all is within you. Do it yourself.

In the Crowley-Harris version of the Tarot, the Hierophant is portrayed with the Goddess beneath him as the source of his power. One could write an entire volume on this theme but for our present purposes this shows a right mating between the right and left hand hemispheres of the brain, and between the masculine and feminine which co-exist in each and every human being. We must become aware of and listen to the deepest and noblest eruption of spirit within us.

We understand our spirit by flowing with our Nature, as fully demonstrated by III The Empress, which leads from 3 — Understanding, it will be remembered — to 2, Wisdom. Do what thou wilt shall be the whole of the Law is the obvious commandment for this stage of evolution. It bids water to flow down in seeking its own level, it bids sheep to eat grass and it bids wolves to eat sheep. However, the society in which we have had the misfortune to be living, is so cock-eyed and cack-handed as to encourage and reward unnatural conduct, quite contrary to the instincts of humanity. This is why people actually have to enquire hard as to what constitutes the Will. So unnatural are our times that learned psychologists and philosophers have even doubted whether there is such a phenomenon as the Will or not. As Schiller has it: 'With stupidity, the Gods themselves argue in vain.' All you have to do is resolve to hold your breath for, say, 93 seconds by your watch — and in keeping your word to yourself, you will find out what Will is.

The purpose of Magick, Yoga, Zen, Sufism et al., is so that you can find out what you are here to do and then do it. Even so, a surprising number of people in our benighted times are so cut off from the inner spirit and find talk of Tarot, Magick and Mysticism to be so 'cranky' — as opposed to being sensible techniques for the acceleration of your own evolution — that they ask how to find their own True Will. At least there is a rough and ready rule of thumb technique. We have feelings. If — as the Empress which is Nature declares — if it makes you feel good, do it. If it makes you feel bad, don't do it. That is the best rough guide to the Will and it is accurate in at least nine cases out of ten. This cannot be said for many rules or guides; nor should we forget that there is always in this Universe 'a factor infinite and unknown'.

Golden rules, so-called, should always be weighed and considered carefully. For instance, how does one define 'evil'? The present writer does not believe in the Christian God and by the same token, he does not believe in the Christian Devil. There is no organising force of Evil in the Universe. There is restriction of Nature and there is mess. However, as a rough and ready rule of thumb, if you can only feel good by making other people feel bad, then you are evil.

The Empress reinforces The Star — and the centre piece of The Hierophant — in that the female, the feminine and the womanly are stressed — and rightly. Once again, too much rubbish is talked about this matter. Obviously men and women are equal — but what sane human being has the slightest patience with loony, feminist nonsense? If we rename San Francisco's 'Fisherman's Wharf', 'Fisherperson's Wharf' as has been done, and if we rename my Rothman's cigarettes 'Rothpersons' cigarettes, we will go nowhere and achieve nothing. The same can be said of those humourless, self-proclaimed 'feminists' whose aggressive behaviour and self-consciously masculine 'slob clothes' would disgrace a drunken sailor on a bad night in Belfast. At the same time, any sane man must fight for the right for women to have equal rights socially, politically and economically.

It is typical of our times — which times are fortunately changing — that men and women, who were made for one another, waste so much energy is quarrels and separation. One must return to basics if there is to be any sense here. The trouble with women — let's face it — is that they're silly bitches. The trouble with men — let's face it — is that they're stupid sods. If men and women only understood this simple, basic truth, then we'd all get along a whole lot better.

There is more, of course. We build from a basic truth. As Crowley stated, it is the nature of Man to penetrate as it is the Nature of Woman to enclose. This is certainly true biologically and tends to be true on most other planes as well.

97

'The proper study of Mankind is Man,' wrote Alexander Pope, the most quoted author in the English language after Shakespeare, and obviously Man is a generic term here for Man and Woman, arguably the most fascinating study on Earth. 'Men are stronger, women are tougher,' is just one of the gems one finds. 'If men had the babies, the human race would've died out centuries ago,' is another. As Latin *macho* aficionados never tire of telling one, it is the *cojones* — balls — which make a man: true, yet the paradox is that the testicles are the most acutely sensitive part of the male anatomy. There is also that fine Chinese proverb: 'Men think and ask why. Women dream and say Why Not?'

Again, a treatise could be written on the subject and many have been issued. Here there is only time and space for remarks inspired by The Empress. We learn Her lessons by the study of Nature. For instance, there is a classic Man's problem. The male ego doesn't ask much in life: merely applause for breakfast, an encore at luncheon and a standing ovation at dinner. Unfortunately, most men worthy of winning those trophies from a compliant woman usually get bored with her within a year and run after some heartless bitch.

Equally, there is a classic Woman's problem. It is: why is it that the men I find domestically compatible bore me shitless and the men I find sexually exciting are domestically abominable?

There is also the puzzling problem of female emotional masochism. Why is it that the best advice one can give to a teenage boy who wants to lay a respectable teenage girl is simply to infuriate her mother? Why is it that the best way not to seduce a woman is to turn up punctual to the minute, in a smart suit done up on the middle button carrying a bottle of champagne, a box of chocolates and a bunch of red roses all graced by a soupy, well-meaning beam? It is hardly masochistic for a woman to kick a ridiculous fool like that — but then why might a wise man turn up an hour late for the same girl, reeking of beer and pickled onions, sloppily dressed and blithely oblivious of any suggestion that he might be out of order as he tumbles casually into bed with her? Sensible men do rather wish that women didn't force them into doing that sort of thing, amusing though it can be on occasion. As a cold matter of fact, most men want to treat a woman well.

It is interesting to consider how well Crowley's opinion has stood the test of time. He thought that all women were motivated by one of three primary drives: The Mother; The Wife; and The Whore. All have their proper function to fulfil and all are worthy of equal respect. The Mother fulfils her Will through her children; the man who impregnates her and protects her nest is secondary. The Wife fulfils her Will through the best man she can find; the children she bears him are secondary. The Whore puts herself first and fulfils her Will by it: both men and children are secondary. This includes career women. But it must be very plainly understood that the term 'Whore' here possesses no derogatory connotation whatsoever. At its best, one is reminded of the eighteenth century English pronunciation, 'hoor', and hence of the divine angels who minister to the warriors of the Muslim Paradise, the *houris*. A whore is simply a free woman who uses her body in accordance with her will. She is on no account to be confused with a prostitute. Though a minority of whores have recourse to professional prostitution when short of money, prostitutes are normally women who do something they don't like for money which they need.

There is for the present purpose a final lesson in The Empress. Both Man and Woman can only evolve by opening up to and accepting Nature and the All-Powerful Female who is present both within us and without us.

At 2 we move from reception into activity. At the most exalted level it is said that only eight men have ever attained to it: Lao-Tzu, Siddartha (Gautama); Krishna; Tahuti (Thoth); Moses; Dionysus; Mohammad; and Perdurabo (Crowley). Each one brought a new Truth for humanity summed up in one Word and each one was misunderstood. Even so, each one had a job to do and did it.

The Two of Wands, Dominion, shows that one word can have the power to shake life on earth to its foundations by altering fundamentally the thinking and feeling of humanity. A beggar dies of dysentery in an Indian gutter — Gautama Buddha — yet his Word ANATTA (No God) alters the life experience for countless millions in the many centuries which come after him. An illiterate ex-camel driver catapulted to the head of an obscure but warlike Arab desert tribe dies saying: 'Please remember I was a man. Just a man,' — Mohammad — yet his Word ALLAH (God) transforms the Middle East and brings civilisation to the West of the dismal Dark Ages. An elderly heroin addict expires from cardiac arrest brought on by a lifetime of dissipated excess in an English residential hotel reminiscent of *Fawlty Towers* — Crowley — yet his Word THELEMA is daily affecting events on the globe as the Berlin Wall falls, the South African government repudiates apartheid and more and more are starting to think for themselves. Naturally, unless we have Dominion over our own thoughts, they will have Dominion over us and we will be slaves, victims of every fleeting whim and passing impulse. This cannot be said of anyone who has ever fulfilled words through action.

'Love is the law, love under will,' as *The Book of the Law* states, so it should hardly surprise us to find that the Two of Cups is Love. For 'There is no bond that can unite the divided but love.' The very nature of the Universe is for each element to seek its opposite. Love is the union of opposites, the union of polarities. If we cannot feel love in our hearts, we will feel nothing very much, thank you. It is the greatest strength in the world other than Will; yet it fulfils Will through its yielding.

The Two of Swords, Peace, shows the stage which comes about when all within and all without are composed to their appropriate stations. This is indeed that Peace of which mystics have spoken, that 'peace...which passeth all understanding.'

Even this does not last for ever. Nothing does, apart, obviously, from Nothing. The Two of Disks reminds us of what we should have known before if we do not realise it now, that the nature of the Universe is Change. This is one reason why that unfathomably wise Chinese Book of Wisdom, the *I-Ching* is also called *The Book of Changes*. All things change all the time. When we can perceive the nature of these changes and align ourselves to them, we can work with them so as to affect all to the advantage of everyone. This is what the Magi do.

There are three Paths to the Supreme in 1 Kether, which is the actualisation of Godhead. The Priestess goes from 6 to 1. On the

Middle Pillar, between Force and Form, between positive and negative, between also the sun of Tiphareth and the Sun behind the Sun (Sirius) in Kether, and uniting them in Love, The Priestess of the Silver Star gives her All to Everything yet remains eternally a virgin. This last may appear paradoxical yet it is not much more than saying that the Universe is in a continuous process of Its own renewal and hence perpetually new every split second.

It is Love alone that can take one through the Abyss. There must be an inner, aching urge for union with the All, as represented by the Goddess NUIT. Only then can one attain HADIT, one-pointed identification in ecstasy with the star one is.

The Magus goes from 3 (Binah) to 1. This experience essentially consists of perceiving the manifested Universe to be an Illusion. Hindus and Buddhists perceive this as Maya, the Great Magus and maker of illusion. One can only respond by concentrating everything into one point.

The Magus also shows the Curse laid upon those who attain to Him. They have to preach the Word for the current state of evolution on earth. They have to teach and enlighten humanity. As if this wasn't a sufficiently thankless and grisly fate, they know also that the truths they utter will be misunderstood and corrupted below the Abyss, that their truths are all illusion, to wit — lies. Yet they still have to do it.

One way out of what could be agony of spirit is to treat the whole thing as a cosmic joke and burst out laughing. If we can't laugh at the sheer absurdity of it all, there is not much hope for our continued sanity. The manifested Universe is the continuous interplay of Love between NUIT and HADIT — the Infinitely Great and the Infinitely Small — and in their continuous copulation is an infinity of joy. As NUIT has it in *The Book of the Law*:

'I am above you and in you. My ecstasy is in yours. My joy is to see your joy.'

And as HADIT states:

'Remember all ye that existence is pure joy; that all the sorrows are but as shadows; they pass and are done; but there is that which remains.'

0 The Fool goes from 2 to 1. At its most exalted, it is too far beyond human conceptions to be rendered capable of description. It is the state known as The Ipsissimus. Nothing sensible can be said about it at all.

However, one can still joke. Who on earth is The Ipsissimus? His/Her Oath forbids the divulging of the fact. One might picture The Ipsissimus in some Tibetan fastness, lost in silent, mystic contemplation. One might picture the Ipsissimus moving stealthily behind the scenes of world events so as to influence them. These charmingly romantic notions may be course be true: but it is vital to remember that it is equally likely that The Ipsissimus is a potato farmer in Iowa. Equally well, he might be living next door to you.

On a lower level reflecting this supreme state, The Fool is an ecstatic state of going. Everything changes, everything goes. It's all go from the start. One can feel it as a gigantic spasm of divinely enraptured intoxication.

At 1, there are the Four Aces — pure energy.

In Kether, Will, Love, Mind and Body are a blazing unity in the star one is within the body of NUIT.

What lies beyond? The Tarot doesn't tell us. Here we go beyond the Word and the Fool. The Qabalists speak of the Three Veils of the Negative; Ain Soph Aour, Ain Soph and Ain — Limitless Light, Without Limit and Nothing.

The ultimate fate of each and every star is succinctly stated in *The Book of the Law.*

'There is the dissolution and eternal ecstasy in the kisses of Nu.'

Epilogue

One might well ask, having drawn all to a point and annihilated It in Infinite Space, what is the point of it all?

It is thought by a number that a star goes for countless incarnations in order to experience every atom of Itself in action. It goes to be totally conscious of Itself. In the going, there is joy. The Fool shows it, for The Fool goes for and rejoices in every experience.

It is very interesting but ultimately unproductive to speculate too much about these virtually incomprehensible matters. Everything is a Point-Event and that's that.

Our time would be better spent dealing with ourselves in the here and now on earth. In the Tarot, we have practical tools for improving ourselves and increasing our comprehension of things around us. The Tarot is not the only set but it is an excellent one and its elasticity in relation to other sets is a distinct advantage. Above all else, the Tarot is there to be used.

The reader may be exhausted but the subject is not. This book simply outlines the bare bones of the matter: it is for the student to give it blood and flesh it out. Research is sorely needed into two subjects so deep and complex as to be outside the scope of this treatise: Tarot and Alchemy; and Tarot and the System of Magick known as Enochian. In both areas there are mines of wisdom.

'You're nothing but a pack of cards!' Alice exclaimed in Wonderland; but one would add: '*What* cards!'

May the Tarot aid the reader in going to awareness and enlightenment. May Thy Will be done with Love in the vast and starry Universe in which we live and move and have our going, Space without End, AUMGN.

THE LESSER BANISHING RITUAL OF THE PENTAGRAM

Face East

1 – Touch the forehead, say ATOH (Unto Thee)

2 – Touch the breast, say MALKUTH (The Kingdom)

3 – Touch the right shoulder, say VE-GEBURAH (and the

4 – Touch the left shoulder, say VE-GEDULAH (and the Glory)

5 – Clasp the hands upon the breast, say LE-OLAHM, AMEN (Unto the Ages, Amen)

6 – Make the Banishing Pentagram of Earth (illustrated). Say IHVH. (Pronounced YE-HO-VAU or YOD-HEH-VAU-HEH).[1]

7 – Turn to the South, the same, but say ADONAI.

8 – Turn to the West, the same, but say EHEIEH.

9 – Turn to the North, the same, but say AGLA.

10 – Turn to the East. Extend the arms in the form of a cross. Extend the legs to make the Pentagram of your body. Say:

11 – Before me Raphael;

12 – Behind me Gabriel;

13 – On my right hand, Michael (Pronounced MI-KAY-EL)

14 – On my left hand, Auriel.

15 – For about me flames the Pentagram,

16 – And in the Column stands the six-rayed Star.

17-21 – Repeat 1-5, the Qabalistic Cross.

NOTES ON PERFORMANCE

A – Commence by visualising yourself growing infinitely tall and upward to the stars.

B – Reach out and above with the right hand. See yourself taking Light.

[1] see Aleister Crowley: *Magick*, APPENDIX VII **LIBER 0 vel MANUS ET SAGITTAE**, SUB FIGURA VI section IV for sequence in which pentagrams should be traced with wand.

C – Let the Light blaze upon your brow.

D – At MALKUTH, imagine you have drawn this Light down through your body from top to toe.

E – Ignite it again at the right shoulder and take it to the left, forming an internal Ankh of Light with your head as the loop.

F – 'Say' means 'vibrate' said word in capitals and the Names of the Arch-Angels if you choose. To vibrate is simply to give a word maximum sonic resonance by using your voice. Make it deep and sonorous; or give it the pitch of the humming-bird.

G – The four Hebrew Words which accompany the Pentagrams are Hebrew Names of God, to be found in *The Bible*.

H – Let the arm swing naturally, going with all your body, to make big Pentagrams. Imagine these drawn in physical flame or brilliant laser light. As you vibrate the God-Name, visualise the Pentagram blazing.

I – To commence with, imagine each Arch-Angel as a pillar or pyramid of brilliant white light.

J – At (15), visualise the Pentagrams blazing all around you and within you.

K – At 16, visualise the Hexagram, the six-pointed star, on your spine, its topmost and bottom-most points being at crown of head and soles of feet.

L – Success is known by an unmistakeable feeling of cleanliness.

It has been said that daily performance of the Lesser Banishing Ritual of the Pentagram for six months — it takes less than five minutes a day — will radically transform one's life by opening strong and hidden depths of the spirit. The present writer's experience confirms this.

The Pentagram is the divine Star of Mankind.

THE PENTAGRAM   THE HEXAGRAM

APPENDIX B

An explanation of the symbolism contained within the cover painting
by the artist Rag.

The Tarot, called by some, the 'Book of Thoth' is related to the
sphere of Hod on the Tree of Life; the number of which is eight.
Thus, an eight spoked wheel in orange, the colour of Hod, is
portrayed with an eye at its centre. This eye is the Magick Eye
used to build up images on the astral plane, the plane where the
Tarot lives and moves. The eye is also symbolic of the union of
opposites, for the blue lids form the vesica of the Goddess, in the
centre of which is the burning red of the God. Their embrace
produces the purple, representing their balance and perfection in
the form of a child.

The purpose of the wheel is motion and the eye directs this
motion. Together they symbolise the God Hadit, the motive
force of the Universe travelling through the body of the Star
Goddess Nuit who is shown as the background of the night sky.
She has 231 golden stars, each one of which is likened unto
Hadit. 231 is the sum of numbers of the Tarot trumps, 0 to 21.
Also, by English Qabala, 231 is the number of 'circumference', a
word used in 'The Book of the Law' to describe Nuit.

The wings are a symbol of 'going' or flight and are green to
symbolise that the nature of travelling is love, for green is the
colour of Venus, the Goddess of Love. Each wing contains 18
feathers, together making 36, which refers to the decans of the
zodiac or segments of the Goddess through which the Sun God
passes. The serpent eating its own tail shows that this love is
infinite; not bound by any one particular form. It is love
beyond form.

It is now seen that this 'winged wheel with Open Eye' is but
the headdress of the Egyptian God Thoth, patron of Magick,
writing and language which are qualities of Hod. He is, like his
Roman and Greek counterparts, Mercury and Hermes, a messenger. The Tarot is also a message, bringing the answer to our
question or intuition to our reason.

The letters T.A.R.O. can also be written R.O.T.A. which means wheel. They are here used to show the cycle of the elements as they occur in Tetragrammaton and referring to the Four suits of the mirror cards.

T. is Teth, related to ♈, the strangest of the Fire signs and thus is here used as Fire.

A. is Aleph, the babe in the waters of its mother and thus is here used as Water.

R. is Resh, the Sun, usually related to Air and thus is used as air.

O. is Ayin, related to ♑, an earth sign. And by its shape the letter symbolises the receptive quality and is thus used to represent the Feminine aspect of Earth.

They appear in the usual colours of these elements each balanced by its correct complementary.

At the top, the number of the Tarot cards, 78 can be seen within a ray of white light. This ray is Mezla, the influence from above, the number of which is 78.

The blackness between the spoke of the wheel is the ultimate void from which All has sprung.

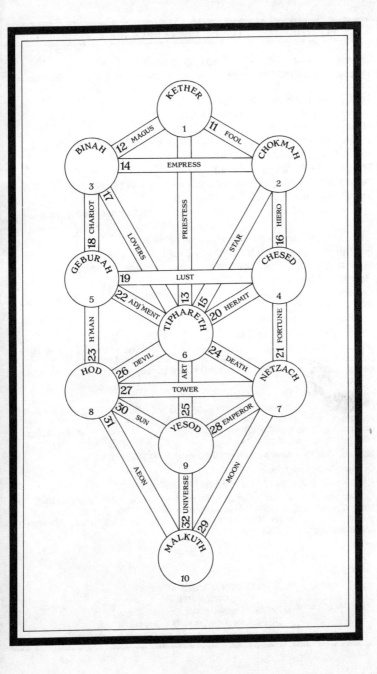

FORTHCOMING TITLES FROM SKOOB ESOTERICA

Michael Harrison: Fire From Heaven
A thorough exploration of the phenomenon of Spontaneous Human Combustion that is not without humour.

The Roots of Witchcraft
Reprint of classic in depth work on witchcraft.

Victor B Neuburg: The Triumph of Pan
Originally published by Aleister Crowley's Equinox Press in 1910. Out now

Three books by Vee Van Dam:

The Psychic Explorer   pbk.
Concerned with astral projection and out of the body experience.

The Power of Mind and Consciousness
Creative visualization, meditation and subjective journeys through inner space.

Star Craft
Discovering auric energies and working with devas.

E Graham Howe: The Mind of the Druid   pbk.
Meditations on the elemental origins of human psychology and faith. Out now.

Gerald Suster: The Truth About the Tarot   pbk.
An illuminating, provocative, and instructive consideration of the tarot. Concise, witty and wise.

Coming from Kenneth Grant

Remembering Aleister Crowley   Illus.
What this memoir of the personal relationship between KG and Crowley in the latter's last years brings to light will change the perspective of occult history. A subtle wisdom and humour informs KG's commentary on their mutual correspondence.

Hecate's Fountain
Often Lovecraftian in ethos, the workings of Grant's Nuit-Isis Lodge have opened the gates to an influx of alien magickal intelligence, which lies behind Grant's revolutionary poetic and scholarly exegesis of Liber Al, and reveals the alchemic potential of our own bodies.

Subsequently the earlier volumes of the two trilogies will be reprinted.

Out now (with Steffi Grant)

Hidden Lore A4 Illus.   Limited to 1000
By their studies of Crowley, Fortune, Spare, Lovecraft and the Tantric tradition the authors have radically altered the direction of the 20th Century Occultism. A distillation in ten essays. With tipped-in colour plates of Steffi Grant's paintings, it constitutes a grimoire. Out now.

SKOOB OCCULT REVIEW
SUBSCRIPTIONS
'Food reading for the thinking occultist.' Pagan News
£10 per Year for 4 issues. Post free in UK.
Please specify issue number you wish subscription to start with.